THE GREEN WAVE: EMBRACING RENEWABLE ENERGY IN MARITIME SHIPPING

BY: Mustafa Nejem

TABLE OF CONTENT

Chapter 1 INTRODUCTION 3

Chapter 2 EVOLUTION OF MARITIME SHIPPING 5

Chapter 3 RENEWABLE ENERGY OPTIONS..8

Chapter 4 TECHNOLOGICAL ADVANCES IN CLEAN PROPULSION............16

Chapter 5 SUSTAINABLE SHIP DESIGN AND RETROFITTING.......................24

Chapter 6 THE ECONOMICS OF GREEN SHIPPING...30

Chapter 7 ENVIRONMENTAL REGULATIONS AND COMPLIANCE 36

Chapter 8 CASE STUDIES IN SUSTAINABLE SHIPPING 41

Chapter 9 OVERCOMING CHALLENGES AND BARRIERS 48

Chapter 10 GREEN PORTS AND INFRASTRUCTURE..55

Chapter 11 MARITIME LOGISTICS AND EFFICIENCY 61

Chapter 12 ENERGY STORAGE AND MANAGEMENT 93

Chapter 13 ENVIRONMENTAL IMPACT ASSESSMENT 114

Chapter 14 MARITIME EDUCATION AND WORKFORCE DEVELOPMENT................122

Chapter 15 GLOBAL COLLABORATION FOR SUSTAINABLE SHIPPING 126

Chapter 16 FUTURE TRENDS AND ECHNOLOGICAL INNOVATIONS.........................131

Chapter 17 ENVIRONMENTAL REPORTING AND ACCOUNTABILITY 136

Chapter 18 GREEN SHIPPING IN A CHANGING CLIMATE................................149

Chapter 19 PUBLIC PERCEPTION AND CONSUMER DEMAND..................................154

Chapter 20 CONCLUSION AND CALL TO ACTION 167

Chapter 1

INTRODUCTION

In the vast expanse of our interconnected world, the maritime shipping industry stands as a behemoth of global commerce, bridging continents and economies. However, this industry, which has been the lifeblood of international trade, faces a profound reckoning—an imperative for transformation. As we embark on this journey through the pages of "The Green Wave: Embracing Renewable Energy in Maritime Shipping," we confront the undeniable need for renewable energy solutions within the maritime realm.

The urgency of this transformation is underscored by a stark reality: the environmental impact of conventional shipping practices. For decades, the seas have borne witness to the relentless use of fossil fuels, resulting in consequences. Carbon emissions from ships have contributed significantly to global warming, while marine ecosystems have endured the collateral damage of oil spills and pollution. In these opening chapters, we peel back the layers of these environmental burdens, revealing a stark portrait of the industry's ecological footprint.

Beyond illuminating the problems, we chart a course toward solutions. The objectives of this book are threefold: to inform, to inspire, and to guide. We seek to educate our readers about the gravity of the challenges faced by maritime shipping today, to encourage a collective shift in mindset towards sustainability, and to guide stakeholders on the path to embracing renewable energy alternatives. To navigate this critical journey, it's essential to understand the book's structure—a roadmap to discovery, change, and a more sustainable future.

This book unfolds as a series of chapters, each meticulously crafted to explore a facet of the transition from conventional practices to renewable energy in maritime shipping. In the following chapters, we will delve into renewable energy options, technological innovations in propulsion, sustainable ship design, and retrofitting. We will scrutinise the economics of embracing greener practices, examine the complex web of environmental regulations and compliance, and showcase real-world success stories from leading shipping companies. Additionally, we will address the challenges and barriers we must surmount, examine the role of green ports and infrastructure, and explore the intricate landscape of maritime logistics and efficiency.

As we traverse these chapters, we will also delve into topics like energy storage, environmental impact assessment, workforce development, and the vast expanse of our interconnected world; the maritime shipping industry stands as a behemoth of global commerce, bridging continents and economies. However, this industry, which has been the lifeblood of international trade, faces a profound reckoning—an imperative for transformation. As we embark on this journey through the pages of "**The Green Wave: Embracing Renewable Energy in Maritime**

Shipping," we confront the undeniable need for renewable energy solutions within the maritime realm.

The urgency of this transformation is underscored by a stark reality: the environmental impact of conventional shipping practices. For decades, the seas have borne witness to the relentless use of fossil fuels, resulting in consequences. Carbon emissions from ships have contributed significantly to global warming, while marine ecosystems have endured the collateral damage of oil spills and pollution. In these opening chapters, we peel back the layers of these environmental burdens, revealing a stark portrait of the industry's ecological footprint.

Beyond illuminating the problems, we chart a course toward solutions. The objectives of this book are threefold: to inform, to inspire, and to guide. We seek to educate our readers about the gravity of the challenges many global collaborations face for sustainable shipping. We will peer into the future, exploring emerging trends and technologies, the importance of environmental reporting and accountability, and the role of shipping in mitigating climate change. We will even delve into the realm of public perception and consumer demand, recognising that the choices of consumers and the public play an integral role in steering the industry toward sustainability.

Each chapter aims to equip readers with knowledge, insights, and a renewed sense of purpose. Our collective journey is not just an exploration of problems and solutions; it's a call to action. It's a call to embrace change, to envision a maritime industry that operates in harmony with our planet, and to understand that the choices we make today will ripple through the oceans and generations to come.

So, let us embark on this voyage together, with open hearts and open minds, as we navigate "The Green Wave" and set sail towards a brighter, cleaner, and more sustainable future for maritime shipping.

Chapter 2

EVOLUTION OF MARITIME SHIPPING

In the annals of human history, the evolution of maritime shipping stands as a testament to our ingenuity and capacity for exploration. This chapter embarks on a captivating journey through time, tracing the historical context and remarkable evolution of shipping from its humble origins to the towering juggernaut it is today. As we delve into the past, we'll unravel the compelling narrative of an industry that has shaped nations, connected cultures, and revolutionised trade.

HISTORICAL CONTEXT AND EVOLUTION OF SHIPPING

Our voyage through maritime history takes us back to the dawn of human civilisation, where waterways were the original highways of exploration and commerce. It is a story of daring adventurers, ingenious shipbuilders, and the relentless quest to connect distant shores.

The tale begins in the mists of antiquity when intrepid seafarers fashioned primitive rafts and dugout canoes, embarking on perilous journeys across rivers and seas. These humble vessels, guided by the stars and the knowledge of coastal landmarks, laid the foundation for humanity's maritime aspirations.

As time flowed like a river into the annals of history, we witnessed the emergence of more sophisticated vessels. The Egyptians harnessed the mighty Nile, constructing sturdy wooden boats capable of carrying precious cargo. The Phoenicians, renowned as master shipbuilders, took to the Mediterranean, creating graceful vessels that ventured beyond the horizon, establishing some of the world's earliest trade routes.

In the age of exploration, iconic figures like Christopher Columbus and Ferdinand Magellan set sail aboard caravels, pushing the boundaries of the known world. Their voyages not only revealed new continents but also reshaped the destiny of nations. The Age of Sail saw the rise of majestic galleons, bristling with cannons and billowing with canvas, as empires competed for maritime supremacy.

By the 19th century, steam power emerged, revolutionising maritime travel. Paddle-wheelers and steamships chugged along rivers and across oceans, making previously unimaginable journeys feasible. The world shrank as ships adopted these new propulsion technologies, opening up global trade and cultural exchange opportunities.

In the early 20th century, steel-hulled vessels and the widespread adoption of internal combustion engines marked a dramatic shift. These technological marvels made maritime shipping faster and more efficient and paved the way for the colossal container ships of today.

These giants of the sea can carry thousands of standard-sized containers, transforming the logistics of international trade.

The maritime sector's evolution is a testament to human innovation and determination. It's a story of progress, exploration, and adaptation, from reed boats on the Euphrates to modern cargo behemoths. Yet, as we delve deeper into this narrative, we find ourselves at a crossroads. The industry's historical trajectory, marred by environmental costs, beckons us to explore greener horizons—renewable energy solutions that can propel us toward a more sustainable maritime future.

THE DOMINANCE OF FOSSIL FUELS

As our narrative progresses through the annals of maritime history, a defining chapter emerges—the era of fossil fuels. This pivotal period marked an unprecedented shift in how ships were powered, transforming maritime transportation and underpinning a globalised world.

The 19th century heralded the dawn of the steam engine era, igniting the maritime sector's fervour for innovation. Steamships, crowned by towering smokestacks, chugged across oceans with inexhaustible power. Coal, the black gold of the industrial age, became the lifeblood of these vessels. Heralding a new age of maritime travel, steamships shattered the limitations of wind and muscle power, offering predictability, speed, and reliability.

The internal combustion engine, an engineering marvel, eventually eclipsed the steam engine. Born in the crucible of the industrial revolution, it brought forth a paradigm shift in propulsion. Early diesel engines heralded an age of greater efficiency and versatility. As a cascade of oil discoveries unfolded across the globe, the maritime industry found a new energy source—liquid gold in the form of petroleum.

The 20th century witnessed a transformative embrace of oil as the dominant fuel. Diesel engines, characterised by their robustness and efficiency, became the engine of choice for ships. Oil tankers, resembling floating cities of steel, crisscrossed the seas to deliver the lifeblood of the industrial world—crude oil and refined products.

This era of fossil fuel dominance brought unparalleled benefits. Ships became faster, more powerful, and capable of traversing the world's oceans with ease. Global trade flourished, economies surged, and societies prospered. Yet, it also casts an ever-lengthening shadow of environmental consequences.

The maritime sector's reliance on fossil fuels came at a significant environmental cost. Vast quantities of greenhouse gases, including carbon and sulphur dioxide, were belched into the atmosphere. The spectre of oil spills haunted both coasts and open waters, causing ecological devastation. The once pristine seas bore witness to the scars of industrialisation.

As we navigate maritime history currents, we understand the complex interplay between innovation and environmental impact. The dominance of fossil fuels propelled humanity forward, connecting distant shores and fuelling economic growth, yet it also carried a heavy ecological burden. Within this dichotomy, the imperative for renewable energy solutions in maritime shipping emerges—a quest for sustainable progress that we will explore in further chapters.

ENVIRONMENTAL CHALLENGES IN THE MARITIME SECTOR

As the maritime shipping industry scaled unprecedented heights of efficiency and global reach, it also cast an increasingly substantial shadow over the environment. This section casts a critical eye on the environmental challenges that have emerged. We'll explore the far-reaching consequences of the industry's reliance on fossil fuels, from the release of greenhouse gases and air pollution to the ever-looming threat of oil spills.

Yet, even amidst the challenges, we recognise that the maritime sector has always been known for its innovation and adaptability. From the earliest wooden vessels to the sleek, modern container ships, the industry has continuously evolved to meet the demands of an ever-changing world. This context makes the imperative for renewable energy solutions in maritime shipping apparent.

As we navigate the historical currents, we'll gain a profound understanding of the forces that have shaped maritime shipping into what it is today. With this historical foundation, we are poised to embark on a transformative journey, exploring how the industry can chart a course towards a more sustainable and environmentally responsible future. The narrative of maritime shipping, as detailed in this chapter, serves as a backdrop against which we will examine the transition from reliance on fossil fuels to embracing renewable energy alternatives in the following chapters.

Chapter 3

RENEWABLE ENERGY OPTIONS

COMPREHENSIVE OVERVIEW OF RENEWABLE ENERGY SOURCES

In the quest to navigate the maritime industry toward sustainability, the compass points toward a treasure trove of renewable energy sources. This chapter embarks on an illuminating expedition through the diverse landscape of renewable energy, where innovation, ingenuity, and environmental stewardship converge.

Our journey begins by casting a wide net, capturing the full spectrum of renewable energy options available to the maritime sector. We explore the classics, like solar and wind power, which have gained widespread recognition and adoption. Solar energy, harnessed from the sun's radiant power, promises clean, abundant, and increasingly cost-effective electricity. Wind power, with its majestic wind turbines, has demonstrated its potential to harness the kinetic energy of the atmosphere, propelling ships forward with a gentle, eco-friendly breeze.

But our exploration continues. We venture into the ocean's depths to uncover the potential of tidal and wave energy. In this realm, the ceaseless motion of the tides and the relentless surge of waves hold the key to sustainable power generation. Like the oceans' heartbeat, the tides' energy can be tapped to produce electricity. Similarly, the kinetic energy of waves, propelled by wind and currents, presents an opportunity for green maritime propulsion.

Hydrogen, the universe's lightest and most abundant element, beckons as a clean fuel alternative. We dive into the intricacies of hydrogen fuel cells, which promise to emit nothing but water vapour as ships traverse the seas. These fuel cells, driven by the chemical reaction between hydrogen and oxygen, are a beacon of hope in pursuing emissions-free maritime travel.

Intriguingly, biomass and biofuels emerge as potential contenders, offering a renewable path toward reducing greenhouse gas emissions. Derived from organic matter, these energy sources can be harnessed sustainably, potentially transforming waste into power. Biomass-based fuels can be synthesised from agricultural residues, forestry byproducts, and even algae, presenting a multifaceted approach to sustainability in maritime shipping.

ADVANTAGES AND LIMITATIONS OF EACH ENERGY SOURCE

As we venture deeper into renewable energy sources for maritime shipping, it becomes apparent that each option has a unique set of advantages and limitations. It is essential to explore these aspects thoroughly to make informed choices and effectively navigate the waters of sustainable propulsion.

SOLAR ENERGY

Advantages

- Abundant and free source of energy from the sun.
- Low maintenance and operating costs.
- Zero emissions during energy generation.
- Can be integrated into existing ship structures.

LIMITATIONS

- Energy generation depends on sunlight availability, limiting nighttime and cloudy-day operations.
- Solar panels require space and may affect vessel aesthetics.
- Initial installation costs can be relatively high.

WIND POWER

Advantages

- Abundant and renewable energy source.
- Low operating costs and minimal maintenance.
- Proven technology with a long history of use.
- Suitable for both large and small vessels.

LIMITATIONS

- Energy generation is weather-dependent and can vary significantly.
- Wind turbines can be visually obtrusive and may pose navigational challenges.
- Initial installation costs and space requirements for wind turbines.

TIDAL AND WAVE ENERGY
ADVANTAGES

- Predictable and reliable energy sources, following tidal patterns and wave cycles.
- Low environmental impact compared to fossil fuels.
- High energy density in some locations.
- Suitable for coastal and offshore applications.

LIMITATIONS

- Highly location-dependent, limiting deployment options.
- Technical challenges in harnessing and transmitting energy from tides and waves.
- Potential impacts on marine ecosystems and navigation routes.

HYDROGEN FUEL CELLS
ADVANTAGES

- Zero-emission energy production when using green hydrogen.
- High energy density and longer range compared to batteries.
- Potential for quick refuelling, similar to conventional fuels.

LIMITATIONS

- Energy-intensive hydrogen production methods, especially grey hydrogen.
- Infrastructure development for hydrogen storage and distribution.
- Costs associated with fuel cell technology and hydrogen production.

BIOMASS AND BIOFUELS
ADVANTAGES

- Utilises organic waste materials, potentially reducing waste and emissions.
- Compatible with existing internal combustion engines.
- Carbon-neutral or even carbon-negative when using sustainable feedstocks.

LIMITATIONS

- Limited availability of suitable feedstocks in some regions.
- Competition with food production and land-use concerns.
- Energy efficiency and emissions vary depending on feedstock and processing methods.

A comprehensive understanding of these advantages and limitations is vital for maritime stakeholders seeking to transition to renewable energy solutions. By carefully weighing these factors against specific operational needs, vessel types, and geographic locations, shipowners and operators can make informed decisions on the most suitable renewable energy sources for their fleets. Additionally, this comparative analysis underscores the importance of technological advancements and ongoing research to overcome limitations and maximise the benefits of renewable energy options for maritime shipping.

COMPARATIVE ANALYSIS OF RENEWABLE OPTIONS

In the quest to chart a course toward sustainable maritime shipping, a comparative analysis of renewable energy sources is akin to plotting a strategic route on the open sea. Each source possesses unique characteristics, akin to distinct islands in an archipelago, offering various advantages and challenges. As we navigate this comparison, we aim to clarify and guide shipowners, operators, and policymakers in choosing the most fitting renewable energy solutions for their vessels.

SOLAR ENERGY

In the realm of renewable energy, solar power stands as a radiant gem, drawing its strength from the boundless brilliance of the sun. Solar energy is a guiding light toward a greener maritime future, like a ship's compass pointing toward a steady course. As we embark on this exploration of solar power, we are met with a treasure chest of advantages woven into its very fabric.

At the heart of solar energy's allure lies its pristine zero-emission profile. Solar panels generate electricity without releasing harmful pollutants into the atmosphere as if touched by the sun's purity. This environmentally friendly facet is the beacon of hope for a maritime industry seeking to reduce its carbon footprint. Additionally, solar energy boasts minimal operating costs and demands little maintenance, a boon for shipowners looking to streamline their operations.

The adaptability of solar panels further enriches the renewable energy landscape. Like chameleons of innovation, these panels can seamlessly integrate into a ship's structure. They find a home on deck, on superstructures, or even as shading solutions in open spaces. This flexibility in placement enables vessels of varying sizes and designs to harness the sun's energy efficiently. As ships glide through sun-drenched waters, their solar panels bask in the light, converting it into electrical power with impressive efficiency.

However, solar energy also leads us through challenging terrain like treasure maps. It navigates through the labyrinth of daylight hours and weather conditions and therein lies one of its limitations. Nighttime operations and cloudy-day voyages pose challenges to continuous energy generation. It's a reminder that even the sun, unwavering in its grandeur, has moments of obscurity.

Furthermore, there's the matter of the initial investment. Creating a solar energy system aboard a vessel demands a substantial upfront cost. The procurement and installation of solar panels, alongside necessary infrastructure, can present a financial hurdle. Yet, the astute mariner understands this expense is akin to a long-term investment. Over time, the benefits of reduced operating costs and carbon emissions far outweigh the initial expenditure. The ship becomes a self-sustaining, energy-efficient vessel reliant on the sun's abundant rays.

Solar energy emerges as a radiant compass in our maritime journey toward renewable horizons, guiding us toward cleaner, more sustainable waters. It invites us to embrace the sun's boundless bounty, weaving environmental consciousness into the fabric of maritime operations. In the end, the limitations of daylight hours and the initial investment are mere ripples on the surface of a vast, sunlit sea of possibilities.

WIND POWER

In the grand tapestry of renewable energy, wind power unfurls like a magnificent sail, capturing the boundless spirit of the wind. This sustainable energy source has stood the test of time as a trusted ally for maritime endeavours, beckoning vessels toward a greener, more environmentally conscious voyage. As we embark on this journey through wind power, we encounter a tapestry of advantages, each a testament to the enduring promise of the wind.

Its bountiful, renewable nature is at the heart of wind power's allure. Like tides' timeless ebb and flow, the wind offers a constant energy source. It can harness kinetic energy from the atmosphere, transforming it into a steady stream of electrical power. This renewable resource comes at a low operating cost, presenting an appealing proposition for shipowners looking to reduce their environmental footprint and cut operational expenses.

Wind power stands as a beacon of versatility in renewable energy. It's a chameleon of adaptability suited to vessels of various sizes and types. From the elegant lines of sailboats to the formidable presence of cargo ships, wind turbines can find their place on decks, masts, or even within the ship's superstructure. This adaptability unlocks many possibilities, enabling diverse vessels to harness the wind's energy efficiently.

However, like the wind, wind power carries the ever-changing nature of the elements. It's an energy source that dances to the rhythm of weather patterns, subject to the unpredictable gusts and lulls of the wind. The result is fluctuating energy generation, where calm days may necessitate supplementary power sources. Navigating through these weather-dependent nuances requires careful planning and operational flexibility.

Additionally, wind turbines, while elegant in their design, alter the visual landscape of ships. Their towering presence may require navigational considerations, particularly in busy or constrained waterways. The initial investment in wind power systems, including the procurement and installation of turbines, alongside space requirements for their placement, must be carefully weighed against the long-term benefits.

In our maritime quest for sustainability, wind power unfurls its sails as a symbol of promise, inviting us to capture the spirit of the wind and harness it for cleaner, more environmentally conscious voyages. It beckons us to consider the renewable bounty that sweeps across the seas. While it carries the unpredictable nature of the wind, it also carries the enduring promise of a greener maritime future. Wind power's notes may ebb and flow in the grand symphony of renewable energies, but the melody remains harmonious, guiding ships toward a more sustainable horizon.

TIDAL AND WAVE ENERGY

Tidal and wave energy come from the never-ending movements of the ocean. They're like nature's reliable batteries, providing power day and night. These energies are created by the pull of gravity and the winds, making them steady sources of electricity. They're also good for the environment because they don't pollute like fossil fuels. But there are some important things to know about tidal and wave energy.

One great thing about tidal and wave energy is that they're predictable. We can count on them to keep making power. They're also kind to our planet, causing less harm than burning fossil fuels. However, there's a catch. We can only use these energies in some places. They depend greatly on your location, so not all ships can use them.

And there are some tricky parts when it comes to getting this energy and sending it where we need it. This can be challenging and might affect the places where fish and other sea creatures live. It can even change the way ships need to navigate. So, while tidal and wave energy are great, we must be careful about how and where we use them.

HYDROGEN FUEL CELLS

Hydrogen fuel cells work like magic potions, giving us clean energy without pollution when we use green hydrogen. They pack a lot of energy in a small space, so they can make ships go a long way without needing lots of big batteries. Plus, they can refuel quickly, just like filling up a car with gas. But there are some tricky parts to know about.

One fantastic thing about hydrogen fuel cells is that they're super clean. When we use green hydrogen, there's no pollution, which is excellent for our planet. They also have a lot of power packed inside, so ships can travel long distances without stopping to recharge. And when it's time to refuel, it's as quick as filling up a car at a gas station.

But there's a catch. Making hydrogen can be hard work and not very green if we don't do it correctly. Some ways to make hydrogen use a lot of energy and can harm the environment. We also need unique places to store and safely deliver hydrogen, which can be a tricky puzzle. And lastly, hydrogen fuel cell technology can be expensive. So, while they're a powerful and clean option, we must figure out these challenges to make them work for ships.

BIOMASS AND BIOFUELS

Biomass and biofuels are like nature's recycling program, turning organic waste into eco-friendly energy. They're a green path to sustainability because they help reduce trash and pollution. Even better, they can work with our existing engines on ships. But there are some important things to know about them.

One fantastic thing about biomass and biofuels is that they're great for our planet. They take things like crop leftovers, wood scraps, or even algae and turn them into valuable energy. This means less waste and fewer harmful emissions. They can even be so eco-friendly that they don't add extra carbon to the atmosphere – they can be carbon-neutral or, even better, carbon-negative.

But there's a catch. Not all places have the right stuff to make biomass and biofuels. They might only work in some places, depending on what's available. There's also a concern that if we use less land for growing biomass materials, we might have less land for food. This competition for land use needs to be managed carefully.

And one more thing – how efficient and clean these energy sources are can depend on the materials we use and how we process them. Some methods are better than others. So, while biomass and biofuels are a green way forward, we must choose the right materials and processes to make them work well for ships and our planet.

Choosing which island to explore is not one-size-fits-all in the grand atlas of renewable energy options. It hinges on individual vessel characteristics, operational profiles, geographic locations, and sustainability goals. By diligently considering these comparative factors, maritime stakeholders can set sail on a course that aligns with their unique circumstances while steering toward a greener, more sustainable future for the maritime industry. Just as sailors navigate the seas with a keen eye on the stars, this comparative analysis serves as a celestial guide, helping navigate the vast ocean of renewable energy options.

ETHANOL: RIDING THE SUSTAINABLE WAVE IN MARITIME

Amidst the evolving landscape of renewable energy in maritime shipping, ethanol emerges as a promising and increasingly trendy contender. Ethanol offers a renewable and environmentally harmonious solution to power vessels, given that it is derived from organic materials, mainly crops like corn and sugarcane. Let's delve into the world of ethanol and explore its role in shaping a more sustainable future for maritime transportation.

RENEWABLE ORIGINS

Ethanol, often referred to as bioethanol or simply ethanol, is crafted from organic sources through a process known as fermentation. The sugars in crops such as corn, sugarcane, and even certain algae become the raw materials for this green fuel. These sugars are converted into ethanol through fermentation and distillation, creating a clean and renewable energy source.

ENVIRONMENTAL BENEFITS

One of ethanol's standout qualities is its low environmental impact. When used as a fuel, it burns cleaner than traditional fossil fuels, emitting fewer harmful pollutants into the atmosphere. This characteristic aligns perfectly with the maritime industry's growing emphasis on reducing greenhouse gas emissions and improving air quality. Ethanol is also biodegradable, further reducing its environmental footprint.

COMPATIBILITY WITH INTERNAL COMBUSTION ENGINES

Ethanol's versatility shines in its compatibility with existing internal combustion engines, making it a convenient and accessible choice for maritime operators. Ships with these engines often use ethanol without extensive modifications, offering a straightforward transition to a greener fuel source.

CARBON-NEUTRAL OR BETTER

Depending on how it's produced and sourced, ethanol has the potential to be carbon-neutral or even carbon-negative. In some cases, the carbon dioxide released when burning ethanol can be offset by the carbon dioxide absorbed during the growth of the crops used to make it. This closed carbon loop aligns perfectly with sustainability goals.

CHALLENGES AND CONSIDERATIONS

While ethanol brings numerous advantages, it's not without challenges. The availability of suitable feedstocks and land use can be limiting factors, as competition with food production may arise. Additionally, ethanol's energy efficiency and emissions performance can vary depending on the type of crops used, the processing methods, and transportation logistics.

Ethanol's ascent in the maritime field highlights a growing trend toward cleaner and more sustainable energy choices. As ships set sail with this renewable fuel in their tanks, they ride the wave of a greener maritime future. While challenges remain, the promise of ethanol as a viable and eco-friendly energy source bodes well for the industry and the environment, making it a noteworthy trend in the quest for sustainability at sea.

By critically evaluating the advantages and limitations of each energy source and placing them side by side, we empower stakeholders in the maritime sector to make informed decisions. It is through this comprehensive exploration that the path to embracing renewable energy in maritime shipping begins to take shape—a path paved with sustainable, innovative, and environmentally responsible solutions.

Chapter 4

TECHNOLOGICAL ADVANCES IN CLEAN PROPULSION

In the maritime industry's relentless pursuit of sustainability, clean propulsion technologies have emerged as the wind in the sails of green transformation. This section navigates through the latest technological advances, propelling vessels toward a cleaner, more efficient, and environmentally responsible future.

HYDROGEN FUEL CELLS: POWERING THE PROMISE OF ZERO EMISSIONS

Hydrogen fuel cells have gained significant attention as a promising clean propulsion technology. These cells generate electricity through the chemical reaction between hydrogen and oxygen, emitting only water vapour as a byproduct. Maritime applications of hydrogen fuel cells are expanding, particularly in ferries and smaller vessels.

- **Advantages:** Hydrogen fuel cells offer zero-emission operation, quiet operation, and high energy density, making them suitable for vessels requiring longer ranges.
- **Challenges:** Hydrogen storage and infrastructure development remain challenging, but ongoing research and investments address these issues.

BATTERY ELECTRIC PROPULSION: THE ELECTRIC REVOLUTION AT SEA

Battery electric propulsion systems are becoming increasingly prevalent in the maritime sector. Large batteries store electricity for propulsion, enabling vessels to operate with zero emissions while in electric mode.

- **Advantages:** Battery electric propulsion is highly efficient, provides instant torque, and produces no direct emissions, making it suitable for short-range coastal and inland waterway vessels.
- **Challenges:** Battery capacity, charging infrastructure, and range limitations are considerations, but advancements in battery technology are addressing these challenges.

LNG PROPULSION: THE TRANSITION FUEL

Liquefied natural gas (LNG) has gained popularity as a transitional clean propulsion fuel. LNG-powered engines emit fewer greenhouse gases and virtually no sulphur emissions than traditional marine fuels.

- **Advantages:** LNG is readily available, reduces emissions, and requires minimal engine modifications for retrofitting.
- **Challenges:** While cleaner than traditional fuels, LNG is still a fossil fuel and doesn't represent a long-term zero-emission solution.

WIND-ASSISTED PROPULSION: HARNESSING NATURE'S POWER

Innovative wind-assisted propulsion systems, such as rotor sails and automated kites, are emerging to harness wind energy for auxiliary propulsion. These technologies can significantly reduce fuel consumption and emissions.

- **Advantages:** Wind-assisted propulsion is a sustainable solution, harnessing wind power to reduce reliance on engines during voyages.
- **Challenges:** Integration and automated control systems are critical for effective operation, and vessel deployment methods vary.

AMMONIA AND METHANOL: GREEN FUEL OPTIONS

Ammonia and methanol are being explored as alternative green fuels. These fuels can be produced from renewable sources and offer the potential for zero-emission propulsion.

- **Advantages:** Ammonia and methanol are energy-dense fuels that can be synthesised using renewable energy sources, offering long-term sustainability potential.
- **Challenges:** The development of safe storage and handling methods, engine modifications, and infrastructure are ongoing challenges for these emerging fuels.

ADVANCED HYBRID PROPULSION: COMBINING THE BEST OF BOTH WORLDS

Hybrid propulsion systems combine conventional engines with electric or alternative power sources. These systems offer versatility, enabling vessels to operate in various modes, including electric-only and emission-reduction modes.

- **Advantages:** Hybrid systems optimise energy use, reduce emissions, and offer operational flexibility.
- **Challenges:** The complexity of integrating multiple propulsion sources and control systems requires careful engineering and design.

WASTE HEAT RECOVERY: TURNING WASTE INTO POWER

Waste heat recovery systems capture and repurpose heat generated by engines, converting it into electricity for auxiliary systems or propulsion. This technology enhances energy efficiency and reduces fuel consumption.

- **Advantages:** Waste heat recovery optimises energy utilisation, making propulsion more efficient and reducing fuel consumption and emissions.

- **Challenges:** Implementation requires engine modifications and careful engineering to maximise efficiency gains.

These technological advances represent the maritime industry's diverse and evolving landscape of clean propulsion. While each technology has unique advantages and challenges, its collective contribution steers the maritime sector toward a greener and more sustainable horizon. As research and innovation continue to push the boundaries of clean propulsion, the industry is poised to navigate a course of environmental responsibility and operational excellence.

DEVELOPMENTS IN RENEWABLE PROPULSION SYSTEMS

Renewable propulsion systems are at the forefront of the maritime industry's transformation towards a more sustainable and environmentally responsible future. This section charts the latest developments in renewable propulsion technologies, propelling vessels toward cleaner and more efficient operations.

WIND-ASSISTED PROPULSION: SAILS, ROTORS, AND KITES

- **Rotor Sails:** Rotor sails, vertical cylinders that spin to harness wind power, have advanced significantly. They are now equipped with automation and control systems that optimise their operation based on wind conditions, vessel speed, and efficiency.
- **Aerodynamic Kites:** Automated kite systems like SkySails have been refined to deploy and retract easily. These kites are capable of generating significant thrust and reducing fuel consumption.
- **Solar and Wind Combos:** Some vessels integrate solar panels and wind-assisted propulsion to maximise renewable energy generation.

HYDROGEN FUEL CELLS: STEAMING AHEAD

- **Advanced Fuel Cell Technology:** Developments in hydrogen fuel cell technology have led to improved efficiency and durability, making them a viable option for larger vessels.
- **Hydrogen Storage:** Innovations in hydrogen storage methods, such as high-pressure tanks and cryogenic storage, enable safe and efficient storage onboard.
- **Hydrogen Infrastructure:** Infrastructure for hydrogen production, distribution, and refuelling is expanding, particularly in ports and coastal areas.

AMMONIA AS A GREEN FUEL: THE AMMONIA REVOLUTION

- **Ammonia Production:** Advances in green ammonia production, using renewable energy sources like wind and solar, have made ammonia a promising alternative fuel.
- **Engine Adaptations:** Marine engines are being adapted to run on ammonia, offering a potential zero-emission propulsion solution.

METHANOL AS A SUSTAINABLE FUEL: GREEN METHANOL PATHWAYS

- **Renewable Methanol:** Methanol produced from renewable sources is gaining attention. It offers reduced carbon emissions compared to conventional methanol.
- **Methanol Retrofitting:** Some vessels are retrofitting their engines to run on methanol, taking advantage of its cleaner combustion characteristics.

BIOFUELS AND SYNTHETIC FUELS: SUSTAINABLE ALTERNATIVES

- **Advanced Biofuels:** Research into advanced biofuels derived from algae, waste, and non-food crops is expanding. These fuels have the potential to reduce emissions significantly.
- **Synthetic Fuels (e-Fuels):** e-Fuels produced through the electrochemical conversion of carbon dioxide and hydrogen are being explored as carbon-neutral propulsion options.

ELECTRIC PROPULSION ADVANCEMENTS: POWER FROM THE GRID

- **Fast Charging Infrastructure:** Ports are investing in fast-charging infrastructure to support the adoption of electric propulsion for ferries and short-range vessels.
- **Battery Advancements:** Lithium-ion batteries continue improving energy density and efficiency, enabling longer electric voyages.
- **Fuel Cell-Electric Hybrids:** Combining fuel cells with batteries in hybrid systems allows vessels to benefit from the high energy density of fuel cells and the instant torque of electric propulsion.

SMART GRID INTEGRATION: OPTIMISING ENERGY USE

- **Smart Grid Technology:** The integration of smart grid technology allows vessels to connect to onshore renewable energy sources, enabling efficient recharging while in port.
- **Energy Management Systems:** Advanced energy management systems optimise propulsion and auxiliary power usage, enhancing overall efficiency.

These developments in renewable propulsion systems are steering the maritime industry toward a more sustainable and environmentally responsible future. With continuous research and innovation, vessels are navigating a course that combines environmental stewardship with operational efficiency, setting sail toward a greener horizon.

EFFICIENCY IMPROVEMENTS AND THEIR IMPACT

Efficiency improvements in the maritime industry are driving a transformation that enhances operational performance, reduces environmental impact, and ensures long-term sustainability.

This section explores the various facets of efficiency enhancements and their profound impact on the maritime sector.

FUEL EFFICIENCY AND EMISSIONS REDUCTION: A GREENER VOYAGE

- **Advanced Propulsion Technologies:** Efficient propulsion systems, such as hybrid engines, waste heat recovery systems, and optimised propellers, significantly reduce fuel consumption and emissions.
- **Cleaner Fuels:** Adopting cleaner fuels, such as liquefied natural gas (LNG) and biofuels, reduces greenhouse gas emissions and improves air quality.
- **Exhaust Gas Cleaning Systems (Scrubbers):** Scrubber systems remove harmful sulphur emissions, allowing vessels to comply with stringent emission standards.

HULL AND HYDRODYNAMICS: STREAMLINING THE JOURNEY

- **Optimised Hull Designs:** Advanced hull shapes, bulbous bows, and air lubrication systems reduce hydrodynamic resistance, enhancing fuel efficiency.
- **Antifouling Coatings:** Innovative coatings deter marine fouling, reducing drag and maintenance requirements.
- **Trim Optimisation:** Dynamic trim optimisation systems adjust a vessel's trim to minimise resistance, improving fuel efficiency.

ENERGY EFFICIENCY ENHANCEMENTS: HARNESSING POWER

- **Waste Heat Recovery:** Systems capture and repurpose waste heat from engines, converting it into usable energy for propulsion or onboard systems.
- **Energy Management Systems:** Advanced systems optimise the use of power, ensuring that energy is allocated efficiently across the vessel's operations.
- **LED Lighting and Energy-Efficient Systems:** Adopting LED lighting and efficient electrical systems reduces onboard energy consumption.

DIGITALISATION AND AUTOMATION: SMOOTHER SAILING

- **Data-Driven Decision-Making:** Advanced data analytics and machine learning algorithms provide real-time insights, enabling more efficient route planning, engine optimisation, and maintenance scheduling.
- **Autonomous Technologies:** Autonomous vessels can operate precisely, minimising human error and optimising fuel consumption.
- **Remote Monitoring and Control:** Remote access to vessel systems allows for timely adjustments and proactive maintenance, reducing downtime.

CARGO HANDLING AND LOGISTICS: EFFICIENT SHIP OPERATIONS

- **Optimised Cargo Stowage:** Advanced stowage solutions enhance loading efficiency and reduce ballast requirements.
- **Just-in-Time Arrival:** Coordination with ports for just-in-time arrivals reduces idle time and fuel consumption.
- **Intermodal Transportation:** Seamless integration with other modes of transportation streamlines logistics and reduces emissions.

COMPLIANCE WITH ENVIRONMENTAL REGULATIONS: MEETING THE GREEN STANDARDS

- **International and National Regulations:** Efficiency improvements help vessels comply with strict emission regulations, avoiding penalties and ensuring access to key trade routes.
- **Sustainable Practices:** Demonstrating commitment to sustainability enhances a company's reputation and marketability.

COST SAVINGS AND COMPETITIVENESS: NAVIGATING THE FINANCIAL WATERS

- **Reduced Operational Costs:** Fuel savings, optimised maintenance, and reduced downtime contribute to lower operational expenses.
- **Competitive Edge:** Efficiency improvements make companies more competitive by reducing costs and offering eco-conscious solutions.
- **Access to Green Financing:** Efficient, sustainable practices often open doors to green financing options with favourable terms.

Efficiency improvements in the maritime industry are not just about reducing costs; they are a strategic response to environmental concerns, regulatory pressures, and market demands for cleaner, more sustainable operations. As vessels become increasingly efficient, they chart a course toward a greener and more prosperous maritime future, ensuring they navigate the waters responsibly and efficiently.

COST-EFFECTIVENESS AND RETURN ON INVESTMENT

In the maritime industry, achieving cost-effectiveness and a favourable ROI is paramount to success. Efficiency improvements and sustainability measures reduce environmental impact and have significant financial implications. This section explores how investments in efficiency and sustainability translate into cost savings and ROI in the maritime sector.

FUEL EFFICIENCY AND COST SAVINGS

- **Cost-Effective Propulsion Technologies:** Adopting advanced propulsion technologies, such as hybrid systems or waste heat recovery, may require initial

investments but results in substantial fuel savings over time. Reduced fuel consumption directly translates to lower operational costs.
- **Emissions Reduction Benefits:** By reducing fuel consumption and emissions, vessels can avoid penalties associated with non-compliance with environmental regulations. This avoidance of fines contributes to cost-effectiveness.

MAINTENANCE AND OPERATIONAL EFFICIENCY

- **Optimised Maintenance Practices:** Implementing data-driven predictive maintenance reduces unplanned downtime, lowers repair costs, and extends the lifespan of critical components. Efficient maintenance practices reduce operational disruptions and associated financial losses.
- **Energy Efficiency Enhancements:** Systems that enhance energy efficiency also reduce operational costs. Examples include LED lighting, efficient HVAC systems, and optimised power distribution, lowering energy bills.

COMPLIANCE WITH ENVIRONMENTAL REGULATIONS

- **Avoiding Penalties:** Compliance with strict environmental regulations is not only a legal requirement but also a cost-saving strategy. Penalties for non-compliance can be substantial, making adherence to regulations a financially prudent choice.
- Marketability and Reputation: Demonstrating commitment to sustainability enhances a company's reputation, attracting environmentally conscious customers and partners. This can lead to increased market share and higher-value contracts.

COMPETITIVE EDGE AND MARKET POSITIONING

- **Attracting Customers and Investors:** Companies that embrace efficiency improvements and sustainability measures often attract investors and partners interested in supporting environmentally responsible initiatives. Access to green financing can provide favourable terms and lower the cost of capital.
- **Higher Profit Margins:** A competitive edge in terms of operational efficiency and sustainability can lead to higher profit margins. Cost-effective operations and a positive public image enhance a company's financial performance.

LONG-TERM FINANCIAL BENEFITS

- **Resilience to External Shocks:** Efficiency improvements, sustainability measures, and adherence to regulations contribute to a company's resilience in the face of external shocks. Whether fluctuating fuel prices, supply chain disruptions, or regulatory changes, a more efficient and sustainable operation is better equipped to weather financial storms.
- **Green Financing Opportunities:** Efficient and sustainable practices open doors to green financing options, often offering favourable terms and lower interest rates. This reduces the financial burden of sustainability investments and improves ROI.

Investments in efficiency and sustainability in the maritime industry are not just ethical choices; they are financially sound decisions. While there may be upfront costs associated with adopting these practices, the long-term cost savings, avoidance of penalties, improved market positioning, and access to green financing options contribute to a positive ROI. The maritime sector increasingly recognises that cost-effectiveness and sustainability go hand in hand, creating a pathway to financial success while charting a course toward a greener future.

Chapter 5

SUSTAINABLE SHIP DESIGN AND RETROFITTING

In the quest for a greener maritime industry, Chapter 5 embarks on a voyage through the fascinating world of sustainable ship design and retrofitting. Here, we explore the innovative approaches and eco-conscious methodologies that reshape seafaring vessels' essence.

Our exploration encompasses eco-friendly ship designs, materials, construction, and the intricate art of retrofitting existing vessels to align with sustainability principles. We'll also delve into real-world case studies that vividly demonstrate the transformative power of these practices.

ECO-FRIENDLY SHIP DESIGNS, MATERIALS, AND CONSTRUCTION

In the maritime industry's journey toward sustainability, the very vessels that ply the world's waters are undergoing a profound transformation. This section explores eco-friendly ship designs, materials, and construction techniques, charting a new course for the maritime sector.

1. **Sustainable Ship Designs: Navigating with Efficiency**

Innovative designs prioritising energy efficiency and reducing emissions are at the heart of eco-friendly ships. These designs encompass various aspects:

- **Hull Shapes:** Modern ship hulls are optimised for hydrodynamics, reducing resistance and fuel consumption. Bulbous bows, optimised propellers, and streamlined hull shapes ensure vessels glide through the water with minimal energy expenditure.
- **Hybrid and Electric Propulsion:** Hybrid and fully electric propulsion systems are gaining prominence. These systems reduce reliance on traditional fossil fuels and offer a pathway to zero-emission shipping.
- **Alternative Energy Sources:** Some eco-friendly ships incorporate wind-assisted propulsion systems, such as sails and rotors, harnessing nature's power to supplement engine propulsion.
- **Energy Recovery Systems:** Innovative technologies like waste heat recovery systems and regenerative braking for ferries help convert energy that would otherwise be lost into usable power.

- **Reduced Emissions Profiles:** Sustainable ship designs aim to minimise emissions through exhaust gas cleaning systems (scrubbers) and low-emission engines, aligning with stringent emission standards.

1. **Environmentally Conscious Materials: Setting Sail with Sustainability**

The choice of materials plays a pivotal role in eco-friendly ship construction. Sustainable materials offer enhanced durability and reduced environmental impact:

- **Lightweight Composite Materials:** Using lightweight composites, such as carbon fibre-reinforced plastics, reduces a vessel's weight, improving fuel efficiency.
- **Alternative Metals:** Sustainable shipbuilding explores alternative metals like aluminium, which offers corrosion resistance and recyclability.
- **Biodegradable Coatings:** Eco-friendly anti-fouling coatings reduce the need for harmful biocides, preventing marine fouling without harming aquatic ecosystems.
- **Recycled and Recyclable Components:** Eco-conscious shipbuilders incorporate recycled and recyclable components, reducing the environmental footprint of ship construction.

1. **Green Shipyard Practices: Constructing a Sustainable Future**

In addition to sustainable ship designs and materials, eco-friendly ship construction embraces environmentally responsible shipyard practices:

- **Reduced Waste Generation:** Sustainable shipyards implement practices that minimise waste generation, focusing on recycling and proper disposal of materials.
- **Energy Efficiency:** The construction process can be made more energy-efficient through optimised manufacturing techniques, lighting, and heating systems.
- **Alternative Power Sources:** Some shipyards use renewable energy sources like solar panels and wind turbines to power their operations, reducing environmental impact.
- **Local Sourcing:** Eco-conscious shipyards prioritise local sourcing of materials and components, reducing transportation-related emissions.

1. **Regulatory Compliance: Navigating the Green Regulations**

Eco-friendly ship designs, materials, and construction techniques respond to market demand and reflect increasingly stringent environmental regulations. Maritime organisations, including the International Maritime Organisation (IMO), are enacting rules that limit emissions and promote sustainability. These regulations drive innovation and adoption of green practices across the industry.

Through these sustainable ship designs, materials, and construction methods, the maritime industry is setting sail toward a greener and more environmentally responsible future. These initiatives reduce the industry's environmental footprint and enhance efficiency and competitiveness. In a world where environmental stewardship is paramount, ship design and construction innovations are guiding the maritime sector toward a new era of sustainability.

RETROFITTING EXISTING VESSELS FOR SUSTAINABILITY

In the maritime industry's pursuit of sustainability, retrofitting existing vessels emerges as a compelling strategy to reduce environmental impact, enhance efficiency, and extend the lifespan of ageing ships. This section navigates the complex and transformative retrofitting process, showcasing how it breathes new life into existing fleets while aligning with environmental goals..

SUSTAINABLE PROPULSION SYSTEMS: A BREATH OF FRESH AIR

A central aspect of retrofitting involves installing sustainable propulsion systems, which are pivotal in reducing emissions and fuel consumption. These systems encompass:

- **Exhaust Gas Cleaning Systems (Scrubbers):** Retrofitting ships with scrubbers is a common approach to reduce sulphur and nitrogen oxide emissions. These systems clean exhaust gases before release, ensuring compliance with strict emission standards.
- **Hybrid Propulsion:** Retrofitting with hybrid propulsion systems combines traditional engines with electric or alternative power sources, enhancing fuel efficiency and reducing emissions.
- **LNG Conversion:** Some retrofits involve converting vessels to run-on liquefied natural gas (LNG), a cleaner-burning fuel that significantly reducing greenhouse gas emissions.

ENERGY EFFICIENCY ENHANCEMENTS: NAVIGATING THE WATERS OF CONSERVATION

Retrofitting for sustainability encompasses various energy efficiency enhancements:

- **Hull Modifications:** Adding air lubrication systems, anti-fouling coatings, and retrofitting optimised bulbous bows contribute to reducing hull resistance and enhancing fuel efficiency.
- **Trim Optimisation:** Dynamic trim optimisation systems adjust vessel trim to reduce drag and save fuel during transit.
- **Advanced Monitoring and Control Systems:** Retrofitting ships with modern monitoring and control systems enable real-time data analysis to optimise engine performance and fuel consumption.

RENEWABLE ENERGY INTEGRATION: HARNESSING NATURE'S POWER

Retrofitting can also involve the integration of renewable energy sources:

- Solar Panels: Installing solar panels on deck areas provides auxiliary power and reduces the reliance on generators.
- Wind-Assisted Propulsion: Retrofitting vessels with wind-assisted propulsion systems, such as sails and rotors, harnesses wind energy to supplement engine power.

WASTE HEAT RECOVERY: TURNING WASTE INTO OPPORTUNITY

Waste heat recovery systems capture and repurpose heat generated by the engines, transforming it into usable energy for onboard systems or propulsion. Retrofitting with these systems enhances energy efficiency and reduces fuel consumption.

SCRUBBER AND BALLAST WATER MANAGEMENT SYSTEMS: ENVIRONMENTAL COMPLIANCE RETROFITTING

To ensure compliance with environmental regulations, retrofitting can include installing scrubber systems for emissions control and ballast water management systems to prevent the spread of invasive species. These systems address regulatory requirements and contribute to sustainability by mitigating environmental harm.

FINANCING SUSTAINABILITY: NAVIGATING THE FINANCIAL WATERS

Financing retrofitting projects can be a complex process. Companies often seek financial incentives, grants, and loans from governments, international organisations, and financial institutions. These financial mechanisms help reduce the financial burden of retrofitting while promoting sustainability.

CASE STUDIES IN SUSTAINABLE RETROFITTING: PROVEN SUCCESS STORIES

Real-world case studies inspire, showcasing how retrofitting can yield substantial environmental and financial benefits. These examples illustrate how retrofitting projects have revitalised existing vessels, reduced emissions, and improved fuel efficiency, all while extending their operational lifespan.

A SUSTAINABLE VOYAGE AHEAD: THE TRANSFORMATIVE POWER OF RETROFITTING

Retrofitting existing vessels for sustainability is a transformative voyage that revitalises ageing fleets and aligns the maritime industry with environmental goals. By adopting innovative propulsion systems, enhancing energy efficiency, integrating renewable energy, and ensuring compliance with regulations, retrofitting breathes new life into vessels, reducing their environmental footprint and setting sail toward a greener and more sustainable maritime future. It's a testament to the industry's commitment to legacy and progress, navigating toward a more environmentally responsible horizon.

CASE STUDIES ILLUSTRATING SUCCESSFUL SHIP CONVERSIONS

In the maritime industry's quest for sustainability, ship conversions offer a compelling path to revitalise existing vessels and align them with environmental goals. These case studies navigate real-world examples of successful ship conversions, showcasing how retrofitting and reimagining older ships can lead to remarkable environmental and operational improvements.

1. **The Cruise Liner Transformation: MS Braemar**

OVERVIEW

MS Braemar, a classic cruise liner, embarked on a transformation journey to enhance its environmental performance and adapt to changing regulations.

CONVERSION HIGHLIGHTS

- **Exhaust Gas Cleaning Systems (Scrubbers):** MS Braemar was retrofitted with advanced scrubbers to reduce sulphur emissions, enabling compliance with stringent emission standards in emission control areas (ECAs).
- **Hull Modifications:** Enhancements, including air lubrication systems and anti-fouling coatings, were introduced to improve hydrodynamics and reduce fuel consumption.
- **Results:** MS Braemar's retrofitting efforts led to a 15% reduction in fuel consumption and a significant decrease in sulphur emissions. The ship complied with emissions regulations and became more fuel-efficient, reducing operational costs and environmental footprint.

1. **The LNG Conversion: Fure Vinga**

OVERVIEW

Fure Vinga, a conventional oil and chemical tanker, underwent a groundbreaking conversion to run on liquefied natural gas (LNG), a cleaner and more environmentally friendly fuel.

CONVERSION HIGHLIGHTS

- **LNG Fuel Conversion:** The conversion involved retrofitting the vessel's engine to accommodate LNG fuel, including installing LNG tanks and associated equipment.
- **Emissions Reduction:** Fure Vinga's conversion significantly reduced greenhouse gas emissions, sulphur emissions, and nitrogen oxides compared to traditional marine fuels.
- **Results:** Fure Vinga's conversion to LNG achieved compliance with emissions regulations and positioned the vessel as a pioneering example of sustainable shipping. The reduction in emissions improved the ship's environmental profile, making it a more attractive option for eco-conscious customers.

1. **The Wind-Assisted Retrofit: Maersk Pelican**

OVERVIEW

Maersk Pelican, a container ship operated by Maersk Line, underwent a retrofit to incorporate wind-assisted propulsion technology, harnessing the power of the wind to improve fuel efficiency.

CONVERSION HIGHLIGHTS

- **Rotor Sails Installation:** The ship was equipped with large rotor sails, which harness wind energy to assist in propulsion.
- **Data-Driven Optimisation:** Advanced monitoring and control systems were integrated to optimise the operation of the rotor sails based on wind conditions and vessel speed.
- **Results:** Maersk Pelican's retrofit with rotor sails resulted in a 5% reduction in fuel consumption, demonstrating the potential of wind-assisted propulsion to enhance fuel efficiency in the maritime industry. This successful conversion illustrated how innovative technologies can be integrated into existing vessels to improve sustainability.

1. **The Ballast Water Management Upgrade: USS Hornet Museum**

OVERVIEW

The USS Hornet Museum, a historic aircraft carrier, underwent a retrofit to comply with ballast water management regulations, preventing the spread of invasive species.

CONVERSION HIGHLIGHTS

- **Ballast Water Treatment Systems:** The vessel was equipped with advanced ballast water treatment systems to ensure compliance with international and national regulations.
- **Environmental Education:** The retrofit included educational initiatives to inform visitors about preventing the spread of invasive species and protecting marine ecosystems.
- **Results:** The USS Hornet Museum's retrofit achieved regulatory compliance and promoted environmental awareness among visitors. It served as a model for historic vessel preservation with a focus on environmental responsibility.

These case studies exemplify the transformative power of ship conversions in achieving sustainability goals. Whether through emissions reduction, alternative fuel adoption, wind-assisted propulsion, or environmental compliance, successful conversions demonstrate that existing vessels can be revitalised to chart a more environmentally responsible course while remaining operational and competitive in the maritime industry.

Chapter 6

THE ECONOMICS OF GREEN SHIPPING

In the dynamic world of maritime shipping, sustainability isn't merely an ethical choice; it's also a profound economic consideration. Chapter 6 embarks on a comprehensive exploration of "The Economics of Green Shipping," delving into the complex financial landscape where adopting renewable energy solutions meets the balance sheets of shipping companies. This chapter illuminates the intricacies of cost-benefit analysis, government incentives, subsidies, and the long-term financial benefits that arise when vessels set sail on the path of environmental responsibility.

COST-BENEFIT ANALYSIS OF RENEWABLE ENERGY ADOPTION

In the maritime industry's pursuit of sustainable practices, adopting renewable energy sources is an environmental commitment and a strategic financial decision. This section embarks on a comprehensive exploration of the cost-benefit analysis associated with embracing renewable energy, shedding light on how this transition can navigate the intricate financial waters of the shipping world.

INITIAL CAPITAL OUTLAY: INVESTING IN A SUSTAINABLE FUTURE

The journey begins with closely examining the initial capital outlay required to transition to renewable energy sources. Retrofitting vessels with advanced propulsion systems, installing solar panels or wind turbines, or incorporating energy-efficient technologies demands a financial investment. These capital costs can be substantial, and they require careful consideration.

However, this initial investment must be viewed through a forward-looking lens. It lays the foundation for a sustainable future. While there is an upfront cost, it is an investment in long-term savings and environmental responsibility.

FUEL SAVINGS AND EMISSIONS REDUCTION: CHARTING THE FINANCIAL COURSE

One of the key elements in the cost-benefit analysis of renewable energy adoption is the promise of fuel savings. Renewable energy sources, such as wind, solar, and hybrid propulsion systems, reduce vessels' reliance on costly fossil fuels. These alternative energy sources provide a pathway to greater fuel efficiency and reduced fuel consumption.

As fuel costs remain a significant portion of operational expenses for shipping companies, these savings can quickly offset the initial capital investments. The analysis involves calculating the payback period—the time it takes for the financial benefits, such as fuel savings, to surpass the initial capital outlay.

Moreover, we explore the financial implications of emissions reduction. As governments impose stricter regulations on emissions, particularly in emission control areas (ECAs), shipping companies that adopt renewable energy sources can avoid potentially costly penalties and ensure continued access to lucrative trade routes. Thus, emissions reductions offer not only environmental benefits but also financial advantages.

PAYBACK PERIODS AND RETURN ON INVESTMENT: THE FINANCIAL COMPASS

Navigating the financial waters of renewable energy adoption requires a keen understanding of payback periods and return on investment (ROI). The payback period represents the time it takes for the financial benefits of renewable energy adoption to offset the initial capital investment. A shorter payback period signifies a quicker ROI and a more financially attractive sustainability project.

On the other hand, ROI factors in not only the direct financial gains but also the intangible benefits like improved brand reputation and access to environmentally conscious markets. A favourable ROI is a compass by which shipping companies navigate their sustainability efforts, ensuring that the financial course aligns with environmental goals.

NAVIGATING FINANCIAL UNCERTAINTY: RISKS AND REWARDS

As with any financial voyage, there are risks to navigate. Fluctuating fuel prices and market volatility pose uncertainties for shipping companies. However, embracing renewable energy sources often translates into resilience against these uncertainties. Reduced fuel consumption and lower operational costs serve as financial buffers, insulating companies from the unpredictability of fossil fuel markets.

The rewards of renewable energy adoption extend beyond immediate financial benefits. Reduced operational costs, improved brand reputation, and access to environmentally conscious markets contribute to a company's long-term profitability and competitive edge in an evolving industry.

Through real-world case studies, we illuminate the financial wisdom of renewable energy adoption in the maritime sector. These stories underscore that sustainability isn't just an environmental imperative—it's also a strategic and financially astute choice. By the conclusion of this analysis, readers will have a comprehensive understanding of how renewable energy adoption isn't a financial burden; it's a compass pointing the way toward a future where sustainability and financial success are not mutually exclusive.

GOVERNMENT INCENTIVES AND SUBSIDIES

In the maritime industry's quest for sustainable practices, governments worldwide have emerged as vital partners, offering incentives and subsidies that encourage and accelerate the adoption of green technologies and environmentally responsible practices. This section unveils the intricacies of government support, a driving wind in the sails of green transformation.

FINANCIAL REWARDS FOR ECO-CONSCIOUS INVESTMENTS

At the heart of government incentives lie the principles of rewarding eco-conscious investments in the maritime sector. Governments recognise that transitioning to green technologies and sustainable practices often requires a substantial financial commitment. To ease this burden, they provide financial grants, subsidies, and tax benefits to shipping companies that embark on sustainable initiatives.

These financial incentives reduce the cost of adopting green technologies and make sustainability financially attractive. They serve as a beacon, guiding companies toward environmentally responsible investments that align with their financial interests.

REDUCED REGULATORY BARRIERS: EASING THE PATH TO SUSTAINABILITY

Government support extends beyond financial incentives to regulatory relief. Recognising that regulatory barriers can hinder the adoption of green technologies, governments streamline permitting processes and environmental compliance requirements for sustainable projects.

Reduced regulatory barriers make it easier for shipping companies to navigate the complex landscape of environmental regulations. It's akin to smoothing the path through a regulatory maze, ensuring sustainable projects encounter fewer administrative obstacles.

NAVIGATING THE WATERS OF INTERNATIONAL COOPERATION

The chapter also delves into international efforts to incentivise sustainable shipping practices. Initiatives like the International Maritime Organisation's (IMO) sulphur emissions regulations and the Energy Efficiency Existing Ship Index (EEXI) set global standards and provide clear guidelines for the maritime industry.

These international collaborations ensure that government incentives harmonise with broader sustainability goals on a global scale. They create a level playing field for shipping companies, ensuring that those adopting green technologies are not disadvantaged in international markets.

FOSTERING INNOVATION: GOVERNMENT-INDUSTRY PARTNERSHIPS

In their quest to foster innovation in green shipping, governments increasingly partner with the private sector. These collaborations aim to stimulate research and development, promoting the creation of cutting-edge technologies and sustainable practices.

Government funding and support for research and innovation projects catalyse advancements in sustainable shipping. They encourage the development of new technologies and solutions that benefit individual companies and drive industry-wide progress.

CASE STUDIES IN GOVERNMENT SUPPORT: REALISING SUSTAINABLE DREAMS

The section concludes by diving into real-world examples of government support for green shipping projects. These case studies offer tangible proof of the transformative power of incentives and subsidies. They showcase how shipping companies have successfully harnessed government programs to fund retrofitting projects, transition to cleaner fuels, and align their operations with environmental regulations.

These narratives show that government incentives are not mere financial windfalls but navigational tools guiding the maritime industry toward sustainability. They exemplify that the synergy between government policies and industry actions can foster a greener maritime sector and ensure that green shipping practices become financially prudent choices. As the maritime world continues its sustainability journey, government incentives and subsidies provide a steadfast wind in the sails of progress.

LONG-TERM FINANCIAL BENEFITS FOR SHIPPING COMPANIES

Adopting sustainable practices in the maritime industry isn't solely a moral or regulatory obligation; it's also a strategic financial decision that can set shipping companies on a course toward long-term prosperity. This section explores the enduring financial benefits that await companies committed to sustainability.

FUEL COST SAVINGS: NAVIGATING THE SEAS OF EFFICIENCY

One of sustainability's most immediate and tangible long-term benefits is reducing fuel costs. Sustainable technologies, such as efficient propulsion systems, hybrid solutions, and cleaner fuels, enhance a vessel's fuel efficiency. As a result, companies experience significant savings in fuel expenses over time.

These fuel cost savings aren't just short-term gains; they compound over the years, translating into a more competitive cost structure. In a world where fuel prices are subject to volatility, this financial stability is a valuable asset.

EMISSION REDUCTION BENEFITS: AVOIDING REGULATORY STORMS

As governments worldwide tighten regulations on emissions, shipping companies that adopt sustainable practices and technologies benefit from avoiding costly penalties and fines associated with non-compliance. Sustainability measures help companies maintain access to lucrative trade routes, minimising disruptions to their operations.

Beyond regulatory compliance, emissions reduction can improve a company's reputation and marketability. Environmentally conscious consumers and clients increasingly prefer to work with companies that demonstrate commitment to reducing their carbon footprint. This translates into long-term financial gains through increased market share and business opportunities.

ENERGY EFFICIENCY: A STREAMLINED FINANCIAL COURSE

Sustainability isn't just about reducing environmental impact; it's also about streamlining operations for greater energy efficiency. Sustainable ship designs and technologies often contribute to improved operational efficiency, reducing energy waste and associated costs.

Efficient practices extend beyond propulsion systems and encompass cargo handling and logistics. Companies that invest in sustainable supply chain practices and energy-efficient operations can optimise their resource utilisation, achieving long-term financial benefits through reduced operating costs.

COMPETITIVE ADVANTAGE: NAVIGATING COMPETITIVE WATERS

Shipping companies that lead the way in sustainability gain a competitive advantage in a market increasingly shaped by environmental concerns. They are better positioned to attract environmentally conscious clients and partners, leading to higher-value contracts and potentially higher profit margins.

Moreover, a reputation for sustainability can differentiate a company in the eyes of investors, making it more attractive for capital investment and partnership opportunities. This financial backing can fuel growth and expansion, further contributing to long-term prosperity.

RISK MITIGATION: WEATHERING FINANCIAL STORMS

Sustainability efforts also serve as a form of risk mitigation. By reducing reliance on fossil fuels and adopting resilient technologies, shipping companies can withstand external shocks, such as fuel price spikes or supply chain disruptions.

In an era of increasing climate-related risks and regulatory changes, sustainability becomes a financial safeguard. It helps companies weather unforeseen financial storms and ensures operational continuity even in turbulent times.

ACCESS TO GREEN FINANCING: A CAPITAL WINDFALL

Lastly, companies committed to sustainability often have increased access to green financing options. Financial institutions, investors, and lenders are increasingly interested in supporting environmentally responsible projects and companies. This access to green capital can provide favourable financing terms and lower interest rates, reducing the financial burden of sustainability investments.

The long-term financial benefits of sustainability in the maritime industry extend well beyond initial investments. By embracing sustainable practices, shipping companies can enjoy ongoing fuel savings, emissions reduction benefits, enhanced energy efficiency, and a competitive edge in the market. Moreover, sustainability is a financial safeguard, protecting companies from risks and offering access to green financing opportunities. In the dynamic and evolving world of maritime shipping, sustainability isn't just a moral imperative; it's a wise financial strategy that charts a course toward enduring prosperity.

Chapter 7

ENVIRONMENTAL REGULATIONS AND COMPLIANCE

Amidst the rising tide of environmental consciousness, the maritime industry navigates a complex web of regulations and compliance standards. Chapter 7 embarks on a comprehensive exploration of "Environmental Regulations and Compliance," casting a spotlight on the intricate landscape of international and national regulations that shape the environmental responsibilities of the maritime sector.

Within these pages, we delve into the depths of these regulations, unveil strategies for achieving compliance and surpassing environmental standards, and shed light on the legal consequences that loom over non-compliance.

IN-DEPTH EXAMINATION OF INTERNATIONAL AND NATIONAL REGULATIONS

In the vast and intricate world of maritime shipping, adopting environmental regulations stands as a compass, guiding the industry toward a more sustainable future. This overview sets the stage for our exploration of the intricate landscape of international and national regulations that shape the environmental responsibilities of the maritime sector.

THE GLOBAL IMPERATIVE: INTERNATIONAL REGULATIONS

On the global stage, international regulations serve as a unifying force, transcending borders to address common environmental challenges. The International Maritime Organisation (IMO) stands as a beacon of environmental stewardship, steering efforts to mitigate the impact of shipping on the world's oceans and coastal communities. Within this international framework, conventions like MARPOL Annex VI establish stringent limits on air emissions from ships, reducing sulphur and nitrogen oxides—a vital step in safeguarding our environment.

The Ballast Water Management Convention, another cornerstone of international regulations, addresses the invasive species transported in ballast water, a global challenge as global as the oceans. These international agreements represent the shared commitment of nations and the maritime industry to protect our planet's natural treasures. They offer a universal compass rose, ensuring that environmental standards are upheld consistently on the high seas.

NAVIGATING LOCAL WATERS: NATIONAL AND REGIONAL REGULATIONS

Yet, our voyage doesn't conclude with international waters. The maritime industry must also navigate the intricate currents of national and regional regulations, each as diverse as the coastal landscapes they seek to protect. These regulations are like the changing weather patterns—dynamic, variable, and influenced by unique environmental concerns.

Within these coastal waters, we encounter emissions control areas (ECAs), regions where sulphur emissions face even stricter limits, and ship speeds may be regulated to protect sensitive coastal areas. Coastal nations tailor their environmental obligations to address their specific ecological priorities. Shipping companies must be like seasoned mariners, adept at adapting to these diverse regulatory currents as they voyage through international, national, and regional waters.

A TAPESTRY OF COMPLIANCE: NAVIGATING THE CHALLENGES AHEAD

Compliance with these regulations is more than a legal obligation; it is a complex tapestry woven with technical challenges, operational adjustments, and an unwavering commitment to environmental responsibility. This section explores the strategies employed by shipping companies to meet and exceed these regulations, from innovative exhaust gas cleaning systems to the adoption of cleaner fuels and alternative energy sources.

Moreover, we delve into the significance of environmental management systems (EMS) and sustainability reporting. These are the tools that not only facilitate compliance but also cultivate a culture of continuous improvement in environmental performance. They are the sextants and compasses that guide companies toward excellence in their environmental commitments.

As we journey through the pages ahead, readers will embark on a voyage into the dynamic world of environmental regulations and compliance. Together, we'll navigate the intricacies of these regulations, unveiling their profound implications for the maritime industry and the natural world it traverses. Amid changing tides and shifting winds, compliance isn't a burden; it is a moral and strategic imperative—a pledge to leave our oceans as vibrant and thriving for future generations as they are for us today.

STRATEGIES FOR COMPLIANCE AND SURPASSING ENVIRONMENTAL STANDARDS

As the maritime industry sets sail towards environmental responsibility, compliance with environmental regulations becomes a requirement and an opportunity for innovation and leadership. This section illuminates the strategies employed by shipping companies to meet these regulations and, in some cases, to go beyond compliance by surpassing environmental standards.

1. **Innovative Technologies: The Engine of Compliance**

One of the primary engines driving compliance is the adoption of innovative technologies. Scrubbers, or exhaust gas cleaning systems, stand as a shining example. These systems reduce harmful emissions, including sulphur oxides, enabling vessels to meet strict sulphur emission limits. Essentially, they are the vessels' environmental lungs, cleansing their emissions before releasing them into the atmosphere.

Selective catalytic reduction (SCR) systems are another technological marvel. They reduce nitrogen oxide emissions by converting them into harmless nitrogen and water vapour. These technologies aren't just compliance tools; they are transformation engines, making vessels cleaner, more efficient, and environmentally responsible.

1. **Cleaner Fuels and Alternative Energy Sources: The Green Fuel Revolution**

Another strategy for compliance lies in the transition to cleaner fuels and alternative energy sources. For instance, liquefied natural gas (LNG) is becoming a cleaner alternative to traditional marine fuels. LNG reduces sulphur emissions to negligible levels and lowers carbon emissions, contributing to compliance with environmental standards.

Beyond LNG, the maritime industry is exploring many alternative energy sources, from hydrogen fuel cells to wind propulsion. These technologies offer compliance and a vision of a greener, more sustainable future for the industry.

2. **Environmental Management Systems (EMS): A Navigational Aid**

Environmental Management Systems (EMS) serve as the compass by which shipping companies navigate the seas of compliance. EMS frameworks, such as ISO 14001, facilitate the integration of environmental responsibilities into daily operations. They provide a structured approach to identifying environmental risks, setting objectives, and measuring progress toward sustainability goals.

EMS isn't just about compliance; it's a proactive approach to managing environmental impact. It fosters a culture of continuous improvement and empowers companies to meet and surpass environmental standards.

3. **Sustainability Reporting: Charting Progress**

Sustainability reporting is akin to the navigational charts that mariners rely on. It provides a clear view of progress toward environmental goals. Companies can transparently communicate their environmental performance, from emissions reductions to energy efficiency improvements. These reports serve as a beacon for stakeholders, showcasing a company's commitment to environmental responsibility.

1. **Proactive Measures: Going Beyond Compliance**

While compliance is the baseline, some shipping companies set a higher standard. Proactive measures encompass many initiatives, from voluntary adoption of stricter emission limits to investment in innovative technologies. These measures are not driven solely by regulatory mandates; a commitment to environmental stewardship guides them.

Some companies voluntarily limit their carbon emissions, effectively exceeding regulatory requirements. They become beacons of sustainability in compliance and as leaders in the race toward a greener maritime industry.

In the following pages, we will explore these strategies in greater detail, discovering the innovative and inspiring ways shipping companies navigate the seas of compliance and set sail toward a horizon where environmental standards are not just met but exceeded. Compliance is not a destination; it's a transformative journey towards a cleaner, more sustainable future for the maritime industry and the planet it calls home.

LEGAL CONSEQUENCES OF NON-COMPLIANCE

In the intricate waters of maritime shipping, non-compliance with environmental regulations isn't merely a misstep; it's a perilous voyage into a sea of legal consequences. This section unveils the potential legal ramifications that loom over shipping companies that fail to adhere to environmental standards. It's a voyage with risks, from hefty fines to reputational damage.

1. **Fines and Penalties: The Cost of Non-Compliance**

One of the most immediate and significant consequences of non-compliance is the imposition of fines and penalties. Governments and regulatory bodies often have mechanisms to punish those violating environmental regulations. These fines can range from substantial monetary penalties to the detention of vessels until compliance is achieved.

The financial impact of fines can be severe, affecting a company's bottom line and profitability. It's a harsh reminder that environmental negligence can come at a steep cost.

1. **Civil and Criminal Liability: Legal Crossroads**

Non-compliance can lead shipping companies down the legal crossroads of civil and criminal liability. In cases of severe environmental violations, legal action can extend beyond administrative fines to civil lawsuits and even criminal charges.

Civil lawsuits may arise from environmental damage caused by non-compliance. Affected parties, such as coastal communities or environmental organisations, may seek compensation for harm caused by a company's actions. Such lawsuits can result in significant financial liabilities and damage a company's reputation.

Criminal charges, while less common, can have even more profound consequences. Individuals within a company, including executives and employees, may face legal action if their actions or decisions lead to environmental harm. Criminal convictions can result in fines, imprisonment, and a lasting stain on personal and corporate reputations.

1. **Environmental Damage Claims: Restitution for Harm**

Non-compliance often translates into environmental damage, and those affected may seek restitution. Environmental damage claims can extend to covering the costs of cleaning up pollution, restoring affected ecosystems, and compensating for lost livelihoods.

These claims can be financially burdensome and are a testament to the potential long-term consequences of non-compliance. They highlight the industry's responsibility to meet regulatory standards and prevent harm to the environment and affected communities.

1. **Reputational Damage: Stormy Seas Ahead**

Perhaps one of the most enduring consequences of non-compliance is the stormy sea of reputational damage. In today's interconnected world, news of environmental violations can spread swiftly, tarnishing a company's brand and eroding customer trust.

Reputational damage can lead to lost business opportunities, decreased market share, and challenges in attracting top talent. It can take years, even decades, to rebuild a damaged reputation, making it a cost far beyond non-compliance's immediate financial consequences.

1. **Regulatory Scrutiny: A Watchful Eye**

Non-compliance can also trigger increased regulatory scrutiny. Regulators may subject a company to more frequent inspections, audits, and heightened oversight, which can be resource-intensive and disrupt operations.

Moreover, shipping companies that repeatedly flout regulations may be subject to even stricter future requirements, increasing their compliance burden and potentially affecting their competitiveness in the industry.

The legal consequences of non-compliance are a reminder that adherence to environmental regulations isn't just a matter of obligation; it's a fundamental responsibility. In the ever-watchful eyes of regulators, affected parties, and the public, the maritime industry must navigate a course of environmental responsibility to avoid the turbulent legal waters that wait for those who neglect their duties. Compliance isn't just a regulatory requirement; it's a commitment to safeguarding our oceans and coastal communities for future generations.

Chapter **8**

CASE STUDIES IN SUSTAINABLE SHIPPING

In this chapter, we delve into real-world case studies that illuminate the remarkable journey of vessels and shipping companies toward sustainability. Each case study showcases innovative solutions, inspiring initiatives, and tangible results, illustrating the transformative power of sustainable shipping practices.

PROFILES OF PIONEERING SHIPPING COMPANIES IN RENEWABLE ENERGY ADOPTION

Several pioneering shipping companies have embraced renewable energy adoption in the maritime industry's transition towards sustainable practices. These profiles highlight their commitment to environmental responsibility and innovative solutions.

1. **Maersk Line**

- **Profile:** Maersk Line, part of the Maersk Group, is one of the world's largest container shipping companies. It has been at the forefront of sustainable shipping practices and renewable energy adoption.

RENEWABLE ENERGY INITIATIVES

- **Triple-E Class Vessels:** Maersk introduced the Triple-E class vessels, renowned for their energy efficiency and reduced emissions. These ships utilise advanced propulsion systems and route optimisation for maximum fuel efficiency.
- **Biofuels and Bio-Methanol:** Maersk is exploring biofuels and bio-methanol as alternative fuels, intending to reduce carbon emissions significantly.
- **Carbon-Neutral Pilot Projects:** The company has been involved in pilot projects exploring carbon-neutral shipping, including using wind-assisted propulsion and green energy sources in ports.

1. **CMA CGM Group**

- **Profile:** The CMA CGM Group is a global shipping company committed to sustainability and renewable energy adoption.

RENEWABLE ENERGY INITIATIVES

- **LNG-Powered Vessels:** CMA CGM has invested in a fleet of LNG-powered container ships, reducing emissions and improving air quality.
- **GoodShipping Program:** The company partnered with the GoodShipping Program, which enables ships to use carbon-neutral biofuels on selected voyages, reducing their carbon footprint.
- **Hydrogen-Powered Container Ship:** CMA CGM is involved in developing a hydrogen-powered container ship, demonstrating its commitment to exploring innovative clean energy solutions.

1. **Colour Line**

- Profile: Color Line, a Norwegian ferry operator, is known for its commitment to sustainability and renewable energy adoption.

RENEWABLE ENERGY INITIATIVES

- Plug-in Hybrid Ferries: Color Line operates the Color Hybrid, the world's largest plug-in hybrid ferry. It uses battery power while in port, reducing emissions and fuel consumption.
- Shore Power Connections: The company has invested in shore power connections at ports, allowing vessels to use electricity from renewable sources while docked.
- Environmental Certifications: Color Line holds certifications such as ISO 14001 and ISO 50001, reflecting its dedication to environmental management and energy efficiency.

1. **Scandlines**

- **Profile:** Scandlines is a German-Danish ferry company that has made significant strides in adopting renewable energy solutions.

RENEWABLE ENERGY INITIATIVES

- Hybrid Ferries: Scandlines operates hybrid ferries with battery systems that reduce fuel consumption and emissions during transit.
- Green Electricity Supply: The company sources green electricity for its ferries when docked, further reducing their environmental impact.
- Investment in Sustainable Infrastructure: Scandlines invests in sustainable infrastructure, including modern terminals and eco-friendly vessels.

1. **Wallenius Wilhelmsen**

- **Profile:** Wallenius Wilhelmsen is a global shipping and logistics company that has made substantial strides in adopting sustainable and renewable energy practices.

RENEWABLE ENERGY INITIATIVES:

- **Investment in Fuel Efficiency:** The company has invested in optimising the fuel efficiency of its vessels, employing measures like air lubrication systems and hull modifications to reduce resistance and fuel consumption.
- **Battery-Hybrid Solutions:** Wallenius Wilhelmsen is exploring battery-hybrid solutions for its vessels, allowing them to operate in a more environmentally friendly mode during certain segments of their voyages.
- **Waste Heat Recovery:** The company has implemented waste heat recovery systems, capturing and converting engine heat into electricity, further enhancing vessel efficiency.
- Wallenius Wilhelmsen's commitment to renewable energy adoption and sustainability demonstrates its dedication to reducing its environmental footprint and setting a positive example for the shipping industry as it charts a course toward a greener future.

1. **IKEA Transport & Logistics**

- **Profile:** IKEA Transport & Logistics is the logistics arm of the global furniture retail giant, IKEA. This company has actively embraced sustainability in its shipping operations.

RENEWABLE ENERGY INITIATIVES

- **Participation in the GoodShipping Program:** IKEA Transport & Logistics partnered with the GoodShipping Program, enabling its vessels to run on carbon-neutral biofuels derived from waste materials and used cooking oil.
- **Efficient Supply Chain:** IKEA places a strong emphasis on supply chain efficiency, including optimising container loads, route planning, and intermodal transportation, reducing both costs and emissions.
- **Investment in Sustainable Transportation:** The company invests in sustainable transportation solutions, including electric trucks and green last-mile delivery options.

1. **Grimaldi Group**

- **Profile:** Grimaldi Group, an Italian shipping company, has been dedicated to sustainability and renewable energy adoption for decades.

RENEWABLE ENERGY INITIATIVES

- **LNG-Powered Ro-Ro Vessels:** Grimaldi Group operates a fleet of LNG-powered roll-on/roll-off (Ro-Ro) vessels, significantly reducing emissions compared to traditional vessels.
- **Solar Power and Energy Efficiency:** The company has installed solar panels on some of its vessels and continues implementing energy efficiency measures throughout its fleet.

- **Hybrid Retrofitting:** Grimaldi Group has retrofitted several vessels to incorporate hybrid propulsion systems, further reducing environmental impact.

1. **Ørsted**
- **Profile**: While primarily known for its renewable energy generation, Ørsted, a Danish energy company, invests in sustainable shipping.

RENEWABLE ENERGY INITIATIVES

- **Green Shipping Solutions:** Ørsted collaborates with shipping companies to implement green solutions on their vessels, such as wind-assisted propulsion and sustainable fuels.
- **Offshore Wind Farm Transport:** The company transports wind turbine components to offshore wind farms using eco-friendly vessels, reducing emissions during installation and maintenance.
- **Carbon-Neutral Operations:** Ørsted aims for carbon-neutral operations, aligning its shipping practices with its commitment to renewable energy.

These exemplary companies have placed sustainability and renewable energy adoption at the forefront of their operations. Through innovation, investment, and a strong commitment to reducing emissions, they demonstrate that responsible shipping practices are possible and essential for a more sustainable and environmentally friendly maritime industry. Their actions inspire the entire shipping sector as it navigates toward a greener horizon.

LESSONS DRAWN FROM PIONEERING SHIPPING COMPANIES' EXPERIENCES IN RENEWABLE ENERGY ADOPTION

The experiences of pioneering shipping companies that have embraced renewable energy adoption offer valuable lessons for the entire maritime industry. These lessons highlight the benefits, challenges, and best practices associated with sustainable shipping.

1. COMMITMENT TO SUSTAINABILITY IS PROFITABLE

Pioneering companies have shown that sustainability and profitability can go hand in hand. Investments in renewable energy adoption, energy efficiency, and emissions reduction align with environmental goals and lead to cost savings, enhanced marketability, and access to green financing options..

2. COLLABORATION IS KEY

Successful initiatives often involve collaboration between shipping companies, energy providers, technology developers, and governments. Partnerships enable the sharing of knowledge, resources, and risk, fostering innovation and accelerating the adoption of renewable energy solutions.

3. INNOVATION DRIVES PROGRESS

Innovation is at the heart of sustainable shipping practices. Pioneering companies continuously explore and invest in cutting-edge technologies, such as hydrogen fuel cells, wind-assisted propulsion, and biofuels, to reduce emissions and improve energy efficiency.

4. DIVERSE RENEWABLE ENERGY SOURCES ARE VITAL

Adopting diverse renewable energy sources, including biofuels, wind power, and electric propulsion, allows for flexibility in addressing different operational needs and reducing the environmental impact of shipping.

5. REGULATORY COMPLIANCE IS NON-NEGOTIABLE

Stricter environmental regulations are driving the maritime industry toward sustainable practices. Pioneering companies recognise the importance of compliance with international and national regulations to avoid penalties and maintain access to key trade routes and ports.

6. PUBLIC IMAGE AND REPUTATION MATTER

A commitment to sustainability enhances a shipping company's reputation and attracts environmentally conscious customers, partners, and investors. Demonstrating environmental responsibility through tangible actions is a powerful marketing and branding strategy.

7. CONTINUOUS LEARNING AND ADAPTATION ARE ESSENTIAL

The maritime industry is evolving, as are the technologies and regulations related to renewable energy adoption. Pioneering companies understand the importance of continuous learning, adaptation, and a willingness to embrace new solutions as they become available.

8. DATA-DRIVEN DECISION-MAKING IS CRUCIAL

Data analytics and digitalisation are pivotal in optimising vessel operations for efficiency and emissions reduction. Real-time data collection and analysis enable data-driven route planning, maintenance, and energy management decisions.

9. INTEGRATION OF RENEWABLE ENERGY ACROSS OPERATIONS

Successful companies integrate renewable energy solutions throughout their operations, including vessel design, propulsion systems, cargo handling, and port energy infrastructure. A holistic approach maximises the benefits of sustainability efforts.

10. PUBLIC AND PRIVATE PARTNERSHIPS FOSTER PROGRESS

Collaboration between public entities, such as ports and governments, and private shipping companies is instrumental in advancing renewable energy adoption. These partnerships create an enabling environment for sustainable practices and infrastructure development.

The experiences of pioneering shipping companies provide a roadmap for the broader maritime industry as it navigates the transition to a more sustainable and environmentally responsible future. These lessons underscore the idea that renewable energy adoption is a moral imperative and a strategic and profitable choice for the shipping sector.

ENVIRONMENTAL AND FINANCIAL OUTCOMES OF RENEWABLE ENERGY ADOPTION IN SHIPPING

Adopting renewable energy solutions in the shipping industry yields significant environmental and financial outcomes. These outcomes contribute to a greener, more sustainable future and positively impact a company's bottom line.

ENVIRONMENTAL OUTCOMES

1. **Emissions Reduction:** The primary environmental benefit of renewable energy adoption is a substantial reduction in greenhouse gas emissions. Shipping companies significantly lower their carbon footprint by transitioning from traditional fossil fuels to cleaner options such as biofuels, LNG, or electric propulsion.

2. **Air Quality Improvement:** Using cleaner fuels and technologies reduces the emission of harmful pollutants, improving air quality in port cities and along shipping routes. This leads to better public health and lower healthcare costs associated with air pollution-related illnesses.

3. **Marine Ecosystem Protection:** Reduced emissions contribute to the protection of marine ecosystems. Lower sulphur and nitrogen oxide emissions reduce ocean acidification and the formation of harmful algal blooms, preserving marine biodiversity.

4. **Noise Pollution Reduction:** Electric propulsion systems and wind-assisted technologies produce less noise than traditional engines, reducing noise pollution in sensitive marine habitats and coastal areas.

5. **Compliance with Regulations:** Renewable energy adoption ensures compliance with strict international and national environmental regulations, avoiding penalties and legal consequences for non-compliance.

FINANCIAL OUTCOMES

1. **Fuel Cost Savings:** The transition to renewable energy sources often results in substantial fuel cost savings. Renewable fuels like LNG or biofuels can be cheaper and more stable than traditional marine fuels.

2. **Operational Efficiency:** Energy-efficient technologies, such as waste heat recovery and optimised propulsion systems, reduce fuel consumption and operational costs. This translates to lower voyage expenses and improved profitability.

3. **Access to Green Financing:** Shipping companies embracing renewable energy and sustainability practices may gain access to green financing options with favourable terms, including lower interest rates and longer repayment periods.

4. **Marketability and Competitive Advantage:** Companies that prioritise environmental sustainability enhance their marketability. They attract eco-conscious customers, partners, and investors, which can lead to higher revenues and market share.

5. **Reduced Maintenance Costs:** Energy-efficient systems and technologies typically require less maintenance, reducing downtime and associated maintenance costs.

6. **Regulatory Risk Mitigation:** By proactively adopting renewable energy and complying with environmental regulations, companies mitigate the financial risk associated with fines, penalties, and potential operational disruptions due to non-compliance.

7. **Resilience to Fuel Price Volatility:** Renewable energy sources like wind and solar power are not subject to the same price volatility as fossil fuels. This provides stability in energy costs and reduces exposure to fuel price fluctuations.

In summary, they are adopting renewable energy solutions in shipping, resulting in a win-win scenario, benefiting both the environment and the company's financial health. Reducing emissions, improved air quality, and compliance with regulations contribute to a more sustainable planet, while cost savings, operational efficiency, and access to green financing enhance a company's profitability and competitive position in the industry. These outcomes demonstrate the compelling business case for renewable energy adoption in the maritime sector.

The case studies we have explored in this chapter exemplify the maritime industry's dedication to sustainability and its profound impact on reducing emissions, improving efficiency, and embracing innovative technologies. Through these remarkable initiatives, sustainable shipping practices are proving financially viable and charting a course toward a greener and more responsible maritime future. The lessons learned from these case studies provide valuable insights and inspiration for the broader shipping industry as it navigates toward a more sustainable horizon.

Chapter 9

OVERCOMING CHALLENGES AND BARRIERS

While adopting renewable energy in the shipping industry offers numerous benefits, it has challenges and barriers. This chapter explores the hurdles that shipping companies face when transitioning to cleaner energy sources and outlines strategies to overcome them.

ADDRESSING COMMON OBSTACLES TO SUSTAINABLE SHIPPING

Sustainable shipping is a crucial step toward reducing the environmental impact of the maritime industry. However, several common obstacles can impede progress in adopting sustainable practices. This section explores these obstacles and presents strategies to address them effectively.

1. HIGH INITIAL COSTS

Obstacle: The upfront investment required for renewable energy systems and eco-friendly technologies can be daunting for shipping companies, especially smaller ones.

Solution:

- **Green Financing:** Seek out green financing options, including loans, grants, and subsidies, that offer favourable terms for sustainable investments.
- **Incremental Adoption:** Start with cost-effective, proven technologies and gradually expand sustainability initiatives as financial resources permit.

2. TECHNOLOGICAL CHALLENGES

Obstacle: Some sustainable technologies are in the early stages of development, making their reliability and effectiveness uncertain. Integrating new technologies can also be complex.

Solution:

- **Pilot Projects:** Conduct small-scale pilot projects to test new technologies before committing to full-scale adoption.
- **Collaboration:** Partner with technology providers and research institutions to gain access to expertise and stay updated on emerging solutions.

3. LIMITED INFRASTRUCTURE

Obstacle: Ports and terminals may need more infrastructure to support vessels using alternative fuels, electric charging, or other renewable energy sources.

Solution:

- Port Collaborations: Collaborate with ports and authorities to invest in infrastructure such as LNG bunkering facilities, shore power connections, and waste disposal facilities for eco-friendly technologies.
- Long-Term Planning: Advocate for long-term planning and infrastructure development to accommodate sustainable shipping practices.

4. FUEL SUPPLY CHAIN UNCERTAINTY

Obstacle: The supply chains for renewable fuels can be unreliable and uncertain, affecting the availability and consistency of eco-friendly fuels.

Solution:

- Fuel Supply Agreements: Establish long-term agreements with fuel suppliers to ensure a stable and reliable supply of renewable fuels.
- Diversify Sources: Consider sourcing renewable fuels from multiple suppliers or exploring on-site production options.

5. REGULATORY COMPLIANCE

Obstacle: Evolving and complex environmental regulations require significant investments in emission control systems and cleaner technologies.

Solution:

- Regulatory Expertise: Stay informed about regulatory changes and collaborate with industry associations to advocate for clear and consistent regulations.
- Compliance Strategies: Develop comprehensive compliance strategies encompassing technology investments, crew training, and monitoring systems to ensure regulation adherence.

6. CREW TRAINING AND ACCEPTANCE

Obstacle: Crew members may need more skills and experience to operate vessels equipped with renewable energy systems, and resistance to change can hinder adoption.

Solution:

- **Training Programs:** Implement training programs to equip crew members with the necessary skills to operate and maintain renewable energy systems.
- **Cultural Change:** Foster a culture of sustainability within the organisation, emphasising the importance of renewable energy adoption and involving crew members in decision-making.

7. RISK MITIGATION

Obstacle: Introducing renewable energy systems may introduce operational risks, and the market for sustainable technologies and fuels can be uncertain.

Solution:

- **Risk Assessment:** Conduct thorough risk assessments and develop contingency plans to mitigate potential disruptions.
- **Diversify Investments:** Diversify renewable energy investments to spread risk across different technologies and fuels.

8. COLLABORATION AND INFORMATION SHARING

Obstacle: The maritime industry can be fragmented, hindering collaboration and sharing best practices and lessons learned.

Solution:

- Industry Partnerships: Engage in industry partnerships and forums promoting information sharing and stakeholder collaboration.
- Knowledge Sharing: Share success stories, case studies, and experiences with sustainable shipping practices to inspire and educate others.

Addressing the obstacles to sustainable shipping requires a multi-faceted approach involving financial strategies, collaboration, and a commitment to innovation. While challenges exist, the benefits of adopting eco-friendly practices are clear, including cost savings, regulatory compliance, and a reduced environmental footprint. By proactively addressing these obstacles, the maritime industry can progress toward a more sustainable and environmentally responsible future.

TECHNOLOGICAL, LOGISTICAL, AND CULTURAL CHALLENGES IN SUSTAINABLE SHIPPING

Sustainable shipping practices face a range of challenges, encompassing technological, logistical, and cultural aspects. These challenges can be complex, but addressing them is essential for the maritime industry to transition effectively toward sustainability.

TECHNOLOGICAL CHALLENGES

- **Unproven Technologies:** The maritime sector is exploring emerging technologies such as hydrogen fuel cells, wind-assisted propulsion, and alternative fuels like ammonia or biofuels. The unproven nature of some of these technologies can raise doubts about their reliability and performance.
- **Integration Complexity:** Retrofitting existing vessels with renewable energy systems or implementing new technologies can be technically complex and costly. It requires adjustments to ship infrastructure, power systems, and the training of crew members.
- **Energy Storage:** Efficient and cost-effective energy storage solutions for ships, especially for long voyages, are still under development. Batteries and other storage technologies need improvements to meet the energy demands of maritime operations.

LOGISTICAL CHALLENGES

- **Infrastructure Gaps:** Many ports and terminals lack the infrastructure to support sustainable shipping practices, such as LNG bunkering facilities or shore power connections.
- **Supply Chain Reliability:** The supply chains for renewable fuels like LNG, biofuels, or hydrogen can be uncertain, leading to potential disruptions in fuel availability.
- **Regulatory Variation:** Differences in environmental regulations between countries and regions can create logistical challenges for shipping companies, requiring compliance with varying standards.

CULTURAL CHALLENGES

- **Resistance to Change:** A significant cultural challenge is overcoming resistance to new technologies and operational practices. Crew members may hesitate to embrace change, particularly if it affects their routines or job roles.
- **Skills Gap:** Training and developing a workforce skilled in operating renewable energy systems and sustainable technologies can be challenging, especially when crew members lack prior experience.
- **Organisational Culture:** Embedding sustainability into the organisational culture of shipping companies can be difficult, particularly if it conflicts with established practices or lacks buy-in from leadership.

OVERCOMING TECHNOLOGICAL, LOGISTICAL, AND CULTURAL CHALLENGES

1. **Research and Development:** Continued investment in research and development is essential to refine and prove the viability of emerging technologies.

2. **Pilot Projects:** Conduct small-scale pilot projects to test and evaluate new technologies before widespread implementation.

3. **Collaboration:** Foster collaboration among stakeholders, including technology providers, ports, regulatory bodies, and shipping companies, to address logistical challenges and align efforts.

4. **Training and Education:** Develop comprehensive training programs to equip crew members with the skills needed to operate and maintain renewable energy systems and promote a culture of continuous learning.

5. **Regulatory Advocacy:** Advocate for clear and consistent environmental regulations and standards at national and international levels.

6. **Market Diversification:** Explore multiple sources and suppliers for renewable fuels to enhance supply chain reliability.

7. **Change Management:** Implement effective strategies to overcome resistance to new technologies and cultural shifts within shipping organisations.

8. **Public Awareness:** Educate and engage the public and industry stakeholders about the benefits of sustainable shipping practices to build support and awareness.

9. Addressing these technological, logistical, and cultural challenges requires a coordinated effort from all stakeholders involved in the maritime industry. The sector must overcome these obstacles to achieve its sustainability goals and reduce its environmental impact.

Addressing these technological, logistical, and cultural challenges requires a coordinated effort from all stakeholders involved in the maritime industry. The sector must overcome these obstacles to achieve its sustainability goals and reduce its environmental impact.

STRATEGIES FOR OVERCOMING RESISTANCE TO CHANGE IN SUSTAINABLE SHIPPING

Resistance to change can be a significant barrier, particularly in the context of adopting sustainable practices in the shipping industry. To navigate this challenge effectively, consider implementing the following strategies:

1. Clear Communication and Transparency:

- Ensure that the reasons for change and the benefits of sustainability are communicated clearly to all stakeholders, including crew members, management, and investors.
- Provide regular updates and progress reports to maintain transparency throughout the transition.

1. **Engagement and Involvement:**

- Involve employees and crew members in the decision-making process. Seek their input and feedback on sustainable initiatives and operational changes.
- Encourage ownership and a sense of responsibility among team members by involving them in the planning and execution of sustainability efforts.

1. **Education and Training:**

- Invest in comprehensive training programs to equip crew members with the skills and knowledge to operate renewable energy systems and eco-friendly technologies effectively.
- Highlight the personal and professional development opportunities that come with embracing sustainability.

1. **Leadership Support:**

- Ensure that top leadership, including executives and management, actively supports and demonstrates commitment to sustainability initiatives.

- Leaders should set an example by adhering to sustainable practices and openly endorsing the changes.

1. **Recognise and Reward:**

- Establish a system for recognising and rewarding individuals or teams that actively contribute to sustainability goals and demonstrate a commitment to change.
- Highlight success stories and celebrate milestones to create a positive atmosphere around sustainability.

1. **Address Concerns and Feedback:**

- Encourage open dialogue by creating channels for employees to express concerns, ask questions, and provide feedback.
- Address concerns promptly and provide evidence-based responses to dispel misconceptions.

1. **Change Management Framework:**

- Implement a structured change management framework with clear goals, roles, and timelines.
- Identify organisational change champions who can advocate for sustainability and support their colleagues through the transition.

1. **Psychological Safety:**

- Foster a workplace culture where employees feel psychologically safe to express their thoughts and concerns without fear of retaliation.
- Encourage a culture of experimentation and learning from failures as part of the change process.

1. **Continuous Communication:**

- Maintain ongoing communication about the progress of sustainability initiatives and their positive impact on the organisation, the environment, and society.
- Use various communication channels such as meetings, newsletters, and intranet platforms to keep stakeholders informed.

1. **Long-Term Perspective:**

- Emphasise the long-term benefits of sustainability, including cost savings, regulatory compliance, and reputation enhancement.
- Show that sustainability is not just a short-term trend but a fundamental aspect of the organisation's future viability.

1. **External Support:**

- Seek external support from consultants, experts, or industry associations to provide additional credibility and expertise in driving change.

- Learn from the experiences of other organisations that have successfully transitioned to sustainable practices.

1. **Celebrate Successes:**

- Recognise and celebrate small wins along the journey toward sustainability. These victories can boost morale and motivation.
- Showcase success stories and share best practices within the organisation.

By implementing these strategies, shipping companies can effectively overcome resistance to change and foster a culture of sustainability. This benefits the environment and enhances the organisation's competitiveness and long-term viability in an evolving industry.

Chapter 10

GREEN PORTS AND INFRASTRUCTURE

Green ports and sustainable infrastructure are pivotal in transforming the maritime industry toward a more environmentally friendly and efficient future. This chapter explores the significance of green ports, outlines key strategies for their development, and discusses the integration of sustainable infrastructure within the broader context of sustainable shipping.

THE ROLE OF PORTS IN SUSTAINABLE SHIPPING

Ports are critical hubs in the maritime supply chain, pivotal in advancing sustainable shipping practices. Their significance in sustainability extends to several key areas:

1. Environmental Stewardship:

Ports are essential in reducing the environmental impact of the shipping industry:

- **Emission Control:** Ports facilitate using cleaner fuels, shore power, and emission control technologies, reducing greenhouse gas emissions and improving air quality in port areas.
- **Waste Management:** Effective waste management systems within ports support recycling and responsible disposal practices, preventing pollution of surrounding ecosystems.
- **Energy Efficiency:** Ports prioritise energy-efficient lighting, cranes, and equipment, reducing energy consumption and operational costs.

2. Sustainable Infrastructure:

Ports invest in eco-friendly infrastructure to support sustainable shipping:

- **Shore Power Facilities:** Ports offer shore power connections, enabling vessels to switch to electricity while docked, reducing emissions and noise pollution.
- **Bunkering Facilities:** They provide access to alternative fuels such as LNG (liquefied natural gas) or hydrogen, allowing ships to adopt cleaner energy sources.
- **Dredging and Waterway Management:** Ports maintain navigable waterways through responsible dredging and sediment management, preserving the ecosystem's health.
- **Renewable Energy Integration:** Some ports incorporate renewable energy sources like wind or solar power to meet their energy needs and reduce their carbon footprint.

3. Regulatory Compliance:

Ports play a crucial role in ensuring compliance with environmental regulations:

- Monitoring and Reporting: They often implement systems to monitor vessel emissions and report data to regulatory authorities, ensuring adherence to emission standards.
- Facilitating Compliance: Ports offer facilities for ballast water treatment, exhaust gas cleaning (scrubbers), and waste disposal, assisting ships in meeting regulatory requirements.

4. Facilitating Sustainable Practices:

Ports encourage and support sustainable practices in various ways:

- **Facilitating Efficient Cargo Handling:** Ports optimise cargo handling processes, reducing vessel idling time and energy consumption.
- **Supporting Green Logistics:** Ports integrate sustainable transportation options like electric trucks and railways into their logistics operations.
- **Promoting Eco-Friendly Shipping:** Ports may incentivise eco-friendly vessels by offering discounts, rebates, or priority berthing to ships with lower emissions and environmental credentials.

5. Innovation and Collaboration:

Ports often serve as hubs for innovation and collaboration in sustainable shipping:

- Research and Development: Ports collaborate with universities, research institutions, and technology providers to develop and test innovative solutions for cleaner and more efficient maritime operations.
- Industry Partnerships: They engage with shipping companies, government agencies, and environmental organisations to promote sustainable shipping practices and share best practices.

In conclusion, ports are vital partners in the pursuit of sustainable shipping. Through environmental stewardship, investments in sustainable infrastructure, regulatory compliance, and support for eco-friendly practices, ports contribute significantly to reducing the maritime industry's environmental impact and fostering a greener, more sustainable future for shipping.

INFRASTRUCTURE ENHANCEMENTS FOR RENEWABLE ENERGY INTEGRATION IN PORTS

Ports play a central role in renewable energy integration for sustainable shipping. To effectively incorporate renewable energy sources into port operations and support eco-friendly vessels, several infrastructure enhancements are essential:

1. Shore Power Facilities:

- **Electrical Infrastructure:** Develop robust electrical infrastructure to provide shore power connections for docked vessels. This lets ships switch off their engines and rely on clean electricity while berthed, reducing emissions and noise pollution.

- **Compatibility Standards:** Ensure compatibility with different ship types and sizes, considering various vessels' voltage and frequency requirements.

2. LNG Bunkering Infrastructure:

- **LNG Terminals:** Construct LNG bunkering terminals within ports to supply liquefied natural gas to ships. These terminals should include storage tanks, loading equipment, and safety systems.
- **Bunkering Procedures:** Develop standardised procedures and safety protocols to ensure secure and efficient LNG fuelling operations.

3. Hydrogen Fuelling Infrastructure:

- Hydrogen Production Facilities: Establish facilities for producing and storing hydrogen as a clean maritime fuel. This may involve on-site electrolysis using renewable energy sources or hydrogen import terminals.
- Fuelling Stations: Implement hydrogen fuelling stations at port facilities, ensuring accessibility for ships equipped with hydrogen fuel cells.

4. Renewable Energy Generation:

- **Solar and Wind Installations:** Integrate solar panels and wind turbines within port areas to generate renewable electricity. These installations can power port operations and supply renewable energy to vessels via shore power.
- **Energy Storage:** Invest in energy storage systems, such as batteries, to store excess renewable energy during peak demand or when renewable sources are unavailable.

5. Sustainable Logistics and Transportation:

- **Electric Vehicle Charging:** Install electric vehicle charging infrastructure for port vehicles and trucks, promoting sustainable transportation within the port.
- **Railway Electrification:** Electrify rail transport within port facilities to reduce diesel emissions from freight transportation.

6. Smart Grid and Monitoring Systems:

- **Smart Grid Integration:** Implement smart grid technologies to efficiently manage and distribute renewable energy within the port efficiently, optimising its use.
- **Data Analytics:** Utilise data analytics and monitoring systems to track energy consumption, emissions, and the performance of renewable energy installations. This data can inform decision-making and improvements in energy management.

7. Research and Development Facilities:

- **Test Facilities:** Establish research and development facilities within ports to prototype and test innovative renewable energy solutions, including advanced propulsion systems and alternative fuels.

- **Collaboration Spaces:** Create collaborative spaces for technology providers, researchers, and industry stakeholders to collaborate on renewable energy projects and foster innovation.

8. Eco-Friendly Infrastructure Design:

- **Sustainable Building Practices:** Implement eco-friendly design and construction practices for port infrastructure, including energy-efficient lighting, heating, and cooling systems.
- **Green Space:** Incorporate green spaces, vegetation, and natural habitat preservation in port planning to enhance the overall sustainability of the facility.

9. Collaboration and Standards:

- **Industry Collaboration:** Collaborate with industry associations, government agencies, and international organisations to develop and adhere to sustainability standards and best practices in renewable energy integration.
- **Knowledge Sharing:** Share experiences and lessons learned with other ports globally to accelerate the adoption of renewable energy solutions in the maritime sector.

By implementing these infrastructure enhancements, ports can effectively integrate renewable energy sources, reduce their environmental footprint, and support the transition to sustainable shipping practices, contributing to a greener and more efficient maritime industry.

CASE STUDIES SHOWCASING GREEN PORT INITIATIVES

Case Study 1: Port of Los Angeles, USA

Green Port Initiatives for Sustainable Shipping

Background:

The Port of Los Angeles, one of the busiest ports in the world, has taken significant steps to reduce its environmental impact and promote sustainable shipping practices.

Key Initiatives:

1. **Shore Power Facilities:** The port has invested in comprehensive shore power infrastructure, enabling vessels to connect to the grid while at berth. This initiative has reduced emissions from idling ships and improved air quality in the surrounding area.

2. **Alternative Fuel Adoption:** The Port of Los Angeles has promoted cleaner fuels like LNG and hydrogen. The port incentivises vessels to use alternative fuels, encouraging a shift away from traditional, more polluting options.

3. **Environmental Monitoring:** Robust monitoring systems track emissions, water quality, and wildlife conservation efforts. Real-time data helps the port assess the impact of its operations and make informed decisions.

Outcomes:

- Significant reductions in greenhouse gas emissions and air pollutants.
- Improved air quality in the surrounding communities.
- Attraction of eco-conscious shipping companies and cruise lines.
- Recognition as a leader in sustainable port practices.

Case Study 2: Port of Rotterdam, Netherlands

Innovative Green Port Initiatives

Background:

The Port of Rotterdam, Europe's largest port, has prioritised sustainability and innovation in its operations.

Key Initiatives:

1. **Eco-Friendly Electricity Supply:** The port uses wind turbines and solar panels to generate clean electricity, powering its facilities and supporting shore power for vessels.

2. **Green Hydrogen Hub:** Rotterdam is developing a green hydrogen hub for producing and distributing hydrogen as a clean maritime fuel. This initiative promotes the use of hydrogen-powered ships and trucks within the port.

3. **Smart Infrastructure:** The port has implemented smart grid technologies to optimise energy use and minimise waste, reducing operational costs while increasing sustainability.

Outcomes:

- Substantial reduction in carbon emissions from port activities.
- Emergence as a global leader in producing and distributing green hydrogen.
- Enhanced energy efficiency and cost savings through smart infrastructure.
- Attraction of innovative startups and investments in sustainable technologies.

Case Study 3: Port of Singapore

Collaborative Sustainability Efforts

Background:

The Port of Singapore, one of the world's busiest and most strategic ports, demonstrates how collaboration can drive green port initiatives.

Key Initiatives:

1. **Clean Energy Transition:** The port has partnered with local utility companies to transition toward cleaner energy sources. This includes adopting natural gas for port operations and promoting LNG as a maritime fuel.

2. **Emissions Reduction Goals:** Singapore's Maritime and Port Authority has set ambitious emissions reduction goals, encouraging shipping companies to adopt eco-friendly technologies and practices.

3. **Research and Innovation:** The port collaborates with local universities and research institutions to develop and test sustainable technologies and solutions, fostering innovation in the maritime sector.

Outcomes:

- Significant reductions in emissions and pollutants.
- Attraction of sustainable shipping companies and investments in green technologies.
- Establishment of Singapore as a leading hub for maritime research and innovation.
- Enhanced reputation as a sustainable and eco-conscious port.

These case studies demonstrate that green port initiatives are achievable through infrastructure investments, incentives for eco-friendly practices, and collaboration with industry stakeholders. Ports worldwide can draw inspiration from these examples to pave the way for a more sustainable future in the maritime industry.

Chapter 11

MARITIME LOGISTICS AND EFFICIENCY

Efficiency within the maritime logistics sector plays a pivotal role in advancing the principles of sustainable shipping. In this chapter, we delve into the multifaceted realm of maritime logistics, emphasising its paramount importance in fostering environmentally conscious practices. We will explore how optimising logistics operations has become a linchpin in driving the maritime industry towards sustainability, focusing on the instrumental role of digital technologies, supply chain management, and the implementation of best practices.

The maritime industry's complex and expansive nature necessitates thoroughly examining logistics practices. The very foundation of efficient maritime logistics lies in the seamless orchestration of various elements within the supply chain. This includes efficiently loading and unloading cargo, minimising idle time at ports, and streamlining the transportation process. By enhancing these core aspects, the industry benefits economically and contributes significantly to reducing its carbon footprint.

One of the pivotal enablers of efficiency within maritime logistics is the integration of digital technologies. The adoption of cutting-edge solutions such as Internet of Things (IoT) sensors, blockchain, and advanced data analytics has revolutionised how logistics operations are managed. These technologies offer real-time visibility into cargo movements, enabling better decision-making, route optimisation, and even predictive maintenance to prevent delays and costly breakdowns.

Furthermore, supply chain management plays a vital role in optimising maritime logistics. Sustainable sourcing, procurement, and inventory management practices can reduce waste, energy consumption, and emissions. By establishing partnerships with eco-conscious suppliers and implementing lean inventory strategies, maritime companies can simultaneously improve their efficiency and environmental performance.

As we progress through this chapter, we will also highlight best practices that have emerged as guiding principles for efficiency and sustainability in maritime logistics. These include adopting a "just-in-time" approach to cargo delivery, which minimises storage and handling costs while reducing emissions associated with vessel idling. Additionally, we will explore the importance of collaboration and information sharing among industry stakeholders, fostering a collective effort to streamline processes and minimise environmental impact.

Sustainable Logistics Practices in Maritime Shipping

Sustainable logistics practices are essential in reducing the environmental impact of maritime shipping while maintaining efficient supply chains. This section explores key sustainable logistics practices in the maritime industry:

1. Green Route Planning

In the pursuit of sustainable maritime shipping, one of the most critical aspects is the strategic planning of routes that minimise environmental impact. This section delves into two pivotal components of green route planning: Optimised Routing and Slow Steaming.

Optimised Routing

Adopting advanced routing algorithms and real-time weather data has ushered in a new era of precision in maritime logistics. By integrating these technological tools, vessel operators can chart safer and significantly more fuel-efficient courses. These algorithms factor in many variables, including wind patterns, ocean currents, and even the shape of coastlines, to identify the most economical and environmentally responsible paths.

Through optimised routing, vessels can avoid adverse weather conditions, turbulent seas, and areas prone to congestion. This not only enhances safety but also minimises fuel consumption and emissions, thereby reducing the ecological footprint of maritime shipping. The synergy between technology and environmental stewardship is beautifully exemplified in this practice, as it strikes a harmonious balance between efficiency and sustainability.

SLOW STEAMING

Slow steaming, another cornerstone of green route planning, entails a deliberate reduction in vessel speed to reduce fuel consumption and emissions significantly. This approach, while seemingly counterintuitive to traditional notions of swift maritime transport, has gained prominence for its undeniable environmental benefits.

By adopting slow steaming strategies, vessels can substantially decrease their energy consumption while adhering to delivery schedules. Slower speeds lead to reduced resistance and lower fuel requirements, making it a viable method for curbing greenhouse gas emissions. Furthermore, this practice aligns with the maritime industry's commitment to energy efficiency and emissions reduction, contributing to a greener, more sustainable future.

In essence, green route planning encapsulates the industry's dedication to integrating technology and strategic decision-making for the betterment of our planet. Through optimised routing and the implementation of slow steaming strategies, maritime shipping becomes more environmentally responsible and economically efficient, reinforcing the idea that sustainability and profitability can coexist on the high seas.

2. Port Optimisation:

Efficient port operations are a linchpin in the quest for sustainable maritime shipping. This section explores two crucial facets of port optimisation: Just-in-Time (JIT) Arrivals and Port Call Efficiency.

JUST-IN-TIME (JIT) ARRIVALS

Coordinating vessel arrivals with port operations through JIT scheduling has become a pivotal strategy to combat idling time and minimise emissions, particularly in congested ports. This practice aims to synchronise vessel arrivals with the precise moment when a berth becomes available. By doing so, vessels can avoid the need to anchor offshore and run their engines needlessly, reducing both fuel consumption and harmful emissions.

JIT arrivals demand meticulous planning and real-time communication between ship operators and port authorities. Integrating digital technologies and automated systems plays a vital role in ensuring seamless coordination. This approach aligns with environmental sustainability and enhances the overall efficiency of port operations, as vessels spend less time waiting and more time in productive cargo-handling activities.

PORT CALL EFFICIENCY

Streamlining cargo handling operations within ports is another imperative for reducing energy consumption and emissions. Port call efficiency optimises the entire process, from cargo discharge and loading to customs clearance and paperwork. The objective is to minimise vessel turnaround time, allowing ships to spend less time at the port and more time navigating the open seas.

Efficient cargo handling not only reduces fuel consumption but also lowers the risk of cargo damage, enhancing safety and reducing costs. This optimisation process often requires improved infrastructure, such as more efficient cranes and handling equipment and streamlined administrative procedures.

In conclusion, port optimisation is a testament to the maritime industry's commitment to environmental responsibility and operational efficiency. By embracing JIT arrivals and striving for port call efficiency, the industry reduces its environmental footprint and improves its competitive edge. This synergy between sustainability and profitability underscores the profound transformations in maritime logistics, ultimately leading to a more eco-conscious and efficient shipping industry.

3. CARGO CONSOLIDATION AND OPTIMISATION:

Efficient cargo consolidation and optimisation strategies are pivotal in advancing the sustainability agenda within maritime shipping. This section delves into two key elements: Container Optimisation and Intermodal Transport.

CONTAINER OPTIMISATION

Containerisation has long been the backbone of global trade, and optimising the use of containers can lead to significant environmental and economic benefits. Maximising container capacity reduces the number of vessels required for transportation and lowers the energy consumption and emissions associated with each voyage.

To achieve container optimisation, meticulous planning and loading techniques are essential. The goal is to utilise every inch of container space effectively, minimising empty spaces contributing to inefficiencies. Digital tracking and monitoring systems can help manage cargo loads more efficiently, ensuring that containers are packed to their full capacity without compromising safety or cargo integrity.

Container optimisation reduces shipping costs and the number of vessels at sea, which translates to lower emissions and less strain on marine ecosystems. This practice underscores the maritime industry's commitment to sustainability through smart cargo handling.

INTERMODAL TRANSPORT

Promoting intermodal transport, which combines sea, rail, and road transportation, represents a powerful strategy for reducing the carbon footprint of cargo delivery. By seamlessly transitioning between different modes of transport, intermodal solutions minimise the need for long-haul trucking and reduce its environmental impact.

Intermodal transport is particularly effective for land-based transportation after cargo is offloaded from ships. It enhances efficiency by taking advantage of the strengths of each mode of transport, such as the cost-effectiveness of sea transport and the speed of rail or road transport. This approach reduces emissions, alleviates highway congestion, and lowers road maintenance costs.

Furthermore, intermodal transport fosters collaboration between various transportation stakeholders, creating a network prioritising efficiency and sustainability. It aligns with the broader objective of reducing greenhouse gas emissions and congestion in urban areas.

Cargo consolidation and optimisation are integral to the maritime industry's commitment to sustainability. Container optimisation and the promotion of intermodal transport enhance economic efficiency and contribute significantly to reducing the industry's carbon footprint. These practices underscore the industry's ongoing transformation towards greener and more responsible shipping solutions.

4. ENERGY-EFFICIENT VESSELS:

The pursuit of energy-efficient vessels represents a pivotal aspect of the maritime industry's commitment to sustainability. This section delves into two key strategies: Investing in an Eco-Friendly Fleet and Prioritising Regular Maintenance.

INVESTING IN AN ECO-FRIENDLY FLEET:

The cornerstone of energy-efficient vessels is the conscious choice of ship technologies and propulsion systems. Investing in an eco-friendly fleet involves a deliberate shift towards vessels equipped with advanced propulsion systems designed to reduce fuel consumption and emissions. Two notable examples include:

- LNG-Powered Ships: Liquefied Natural Gas (LNG) has emerged as a cleaner-burning alternative to traditional marine fuels. LNG-powered ships not only produce fewer greenhouse gas emissions but also have the potential to reduce air pollutants significantly. This transition aligns with the industry's commitment to transitioning from more carbon-intensive fuels.
- Wind-Assisted Propulsion: Incorporating wind-assisted propulsion systems, such as sails or rotor sails, can harness the power of the wind to augment a vessel's propulsion. This reduces the reliance on fossil fuels, especially during favourable wind conditions. These systems are often designed to be aerodynamically efficient and can be seamlessly integrated into existing vessel designs.

Adopting these advanced propulsion systems reduces the ecological footprint of maritime shipping and positions shipping companies as leaders in sustainable practices, appealing to environmentally conscious customers and stakeholders.

REGULAR MAINTENANCE:

Maintaining vessels is a fundamental practice in ensuring optimal engine and hull performance. Regular maintenance routines can help identify and rectify issues that may compromise a vessel's efficiency, leading to increased fuel consumption and emissions.

Scheduled maintenance includes engine overhauls, hull cleaning, and inspections to ensure that all systems are in top working condition. Proper maintenance extends the operational life of vessels and ensures that they operate at peak efficiency, ultimately reducing the environmental impact associated with each voyage.

Moreover, maintenance practices also encompass fuel-efficient technologies, such as hull coatings that reduce friction with water or installing energy-efficient lighting and appliances on board. These small changes contribute to overall fuel savings and emissions reductions.

Prioritising energy-efficient vessels through investments in advanced propulsion systems and regular maintenance is central to the maritime industry's drive for sustainability. This benefits the environment by reducing emissions and enhances the industry's competitiveness and resilience in a world increasingly focused on eco-conscious practices.

5. SUSTAINABLE FUELS AND TECHNOLOGIES:

Integrating sustainable fuels and cutting-edge technologies is a pivotal driver in advancing the sustainability agenda within the maritime industry. This section explores two crucial elements: Alternative Fuels and Wind and Solar Power.

ALTERNATIVE FUELS

- LNG (Liquefied Natural Gas): LNG is becoming a sustainable alternative to traditional bunker fuels. It burns more cleanly, emitting fewer greenhouse gases and air pollutants. LNG infrastructure is expanding, making it a viable choice for vessel operators looking to reduce their environmental impact. Additionally, LNG-powered ships are often designed with dual-fuel capabilities, providing flexibility in fuel selection
- Hydrogen: Hydrogen is a promising fuel source for maritime applications. When produced using renewable energy sources like wind or solar power, hydrogen is entirely emissions-free. Hydrogen fuel cells can power vessels, producing electricity on board while emitting only water vapour as a byproduct. This technology represents a significant step towards zero-emission shipping.
- Biofuels: Biofuels, derived from organic matter such as algae or waste products, offer a sustainable alternative to fossil fuels. These fuels can be blended with traditional fuels or used as a drop-in replacement, reducing carbon emissions and promoting circular economy practices.

Adopting alternative fuels aligns with the maritime industry's commitment to reducing emissions and transitioning to more sustainable energy sources.

WIND AND SOLAR POWER

Harnessing wind and solar power for onboard energy generation represents a forward-thinking strategy to reduce reliance on fossil fuels. Vessels can integrate wind turbines and solar panels into their design to generate clean electricity. These technologies can power onboard systems, reducing the need to run auxiliary engines often powered by traditional fuels.

- **Wind Power:** Wind-assisted propulsion systems, such as sails or rotor sails, capture wind energy to assist in propulsion. These systems reduce fuel consumption and serve as a symbol of a vessel's commitment to sustainability.
- **Solar Power:** Solar panels installed on a vessel's deck or superstructure can convert sunlight into electricity. This electricity can power lighting, navigation systems, and other onboard equipment. Solar power is particularly effective in regions with abundant sunshine.

Integrating wind and solar power enhances a vessel's energy efficiency and reduces its environmental footprint, contributing to a greener and more sustainable maritime industry.

Embracing sustainable fuels and technologies is paramount in the maritime industry's journey towards environmental responsibility. By adopting alternative fuels and harnessing the power of wind and solar energy, vessels can significantly reduce emissions, lower operating costs, and position themselves as leaders in sustainable shipping practices.

6. EMISSION REDUCTION TECHNOLOGIES:

Efforts to reduce emissions within the maritime industry are imperative for a sustainable future. We will focus on two key emission reduction technologies: Exhaust Gas Cleaning Systems (Scrubbers) and Emission Monitoring.

EXHAUST GAS CLEANING SYSTEMS (SCRUBBERS)

- Scrubber Technology: Exhaust Gas Cleaning Systems, commonly known as scrubbers, are vital in mitigating sulphur oxide emissions from vessels. These systems work by spraying seawater or specialised solutions into a vessel's exhaust gases, removing harmful sulphur oxides before they are released into the atmosphere. This technology allows vessels to continue using traditional high-sulphur bunker fuels while complying with stringent international emissions regulations, such as the IMO's (International Maritime Organisation) sulphur cap.
- Compliance with Regulations: The installation of scrubbers not only reduces sulphur oxide emissions but also ensures compliance with emissions standards. This is particularly crucial in Emission Control Areas (ECAs) and other regions where strict

limits on fuel sulphur content are enforced. By using scrubbers, vessels can navigate these areas without switching to low-sulphur fuels, which are often more expensive.

EMISSION MONITORING

- **Real-Time Emission Monitoring:** Adopting real-time emissions monitoring systems is pivotal in tracking and reducing vessel air pollutant emissions. These systems continuously collect data on emissions, providing valuable insights into a vessel's environmental performance.
- **Data-Driven Decision-Making:** Emission monitoring systems enable ship operators to make data-driven decisions to optimise engine performance and reduce emissions. By closely monitoring emissions, vessel operators can adjust engine parameters, fuel consumption, and operational practices to minimise environmental impact.
- **Environmental Reporting:** Emission monitoring systems also facilitate transparent reporting of emissions data to regulatory authorities and stakeholders. This accountability fosters a culture of environmental responsibility within the maritime industry.

Implementing emission reduction technologies such as scrubbers and real-time emission monitoring systems is a proactive approach that underscores the maritime industry's commitment to environmental sustainability. These technologies reduce harmful emissions and ensure compliance with international regulations while promoting a data-driven, environmentally responsible ethos within the industry.

7. CARGO TRACKING AND VISIBILITY:

Effective cargo tracking and visibility are integral to enhancing efficiency and sustainability within maritime shipping. This section explores two key aspects: Supply Chain Visibility and Data-Driven Decision-Making.

SUPPLY CHAIN VISIBILITY

- **IoT Sensors:** Integrating Internet of Things (IoT) sensors within the supply chain has revolutionised cargo tracking. These sensors provide real-time data on cargo location, temperature, humidity, and security status. This level of visibility allows for proactive management of shipments, ensuring that cargo is handled appropriately and that any deviations from the planned route or conditions are promptly addressed.
- **Blockchain Technology:** Blockchain technology offers a secure and transparent means of recording and sharing supply chain data. By leveraging blockchain, stakeholders within the maritime industry can maintain an immutable ledger of cargo movements, contracts, and documentation. This reduces the risk of fraud and streamlines administrative processes, leading to faster cargo clearance and reduced paperwork.

Enhanced supply chain visibility reduces inefficiencies, minimises delays, and timely deliveries. By monitoring cargo conditions and locations in real-time, the industry can take proactive steps to optimise routes, mitigate risks, and reduce waste.

DATA-DRIVEN DECISIONS

- Cargo Optimisation: Data analytics plays a pivotal role in optimising cargo loading, unloading, and transport routes. By analysing historical data and real-time information, maritime operators can determine the most efficient way to load cargo, ensuring that vessels are not carrying excess weight or leaving valuable cargo space unused.
- Route Optimisation: Data analytics also informs route planning and navigation decisions. By considering factors such as weather patterns, traffic in congested ports, and fuel consumption data, vessels can chart the most fuel-efficient routes. This reduces energy consumption and emissions while maintaining delivery schedules.

Data-driven decision-making is the hallmark of a modern and sustainable maritime industry. By harnessing the power of data analytics, the industry can continually refine its operations, reduce environmental impact, and adapt to changing market conditions.

Cargo tracking and visibility are fundamental to the maritime industry's quest for sustainability. Leveraging IoT sensors, blockchain technology, and data analytics enhances operational efficiency and reduces energy consumption, greenhouse gas emissions, and overall environmental impact. These technologies usher in a new era of smart, environmentally responsible maritime shipping.

8. ENVIRONMENTAL CERTIFICATION AND STANDARDS:

Environmental certification and adherence to standards are essential pillars of the maritime industry's commitment to sustainability. This section explores two crucial aspects: Eco-Certification and Adherence to Regulations.

ECO-CERTIFICATION

- **Seeking Eco-Certifications:** Maritime companies can actively pursue eco-certifications that recognise their commitment to sustainable logistics practices. These certifications, often awarded by recognised organisations, endorse a company's environmental responsibility. Examples include the Green Marine certification in North America and the ISO 14001 environmental management standard.
- **Enhancing Reputation:** Eco-certifications validate a company's sustainability efforts and enhance its reputation in the eyes of eco-conscious customers, partners, and investors. Customers increasingly seek companies that are committed to reducing their environmental footprint. Eco-certifications can be a powerful marketing tool, attracting a broader customer base and strengthening brand loyalty.

ADHERENCE TO REGULATIONS

- **Awareness and Compliance:** Staying informed about and adhering to international and national environmental regulations is non-negotiable for maritime industry stakeholders. Regulations such as the International Maritime Organisation's (IMO) MARPOL Annex VI set vessel emission limits. Compliance ensures that vessels meet

stringent environmental standards, reducing harmful emissions and protecting marine ecosystems.
- **Proactive Measures**: Instead of viewing regulations as mere compliance requirements, maritime companies can proactively embrace them as opportunities to drive positive change. By exceeding regulatory standards, companies can showcase their dedication to environmental stewardship and set themselves apart as industry leaders in sustainability.

Environmental certification and adherence to regulations are instrumental in shaping a more sustainable maritime industry. Eco-certifications bolster a company's reputation and appeal to eco-conscious customers. At the same time, strict adherence to environmental regulations ensures compliance with international standards and fosters a culture of environmental responsibility within the industry. These practices underscore the maritime sector's commitment to being a responsible custodian of the oceans and the environment.

9. SUSTAINABLE WAREHOUSING AND DISTRIBUTION:

Sustainable warehousing and distribution practices are crucial in reducing the environmental footprint of the logistics industry. This section explores two key strategies: Green Warehouses and Last-Mile Delivery.

GREEN WAREHOUSES

- Energy-Efficient Infrastructure: Green warehouses prioritise energy-efficient infrastructure. This includes adopting LED lighting, advanced heating and cooling systems, and insulation measures to reduce energy consumption. Integrating renewable energy sources like solar panels further minimises the environmental impact of warehouse operations.
- Waste Reduction Measures: Sustainable warehousing involves implementing waste reduction measures, such as recycling programs and waste-to-energy systems. These initiatives minimise landfill waste and contribute to a circular economy. Additionally, optimising inventory management reduces unnecessary waste by preventing overstocking or spoilage of goods.
- Transportation Efficiency: Warehouses can play a crucial role in transportation efficiency by optimising the loading and unloading of goods. Streamlining these processes reduces idle times for delivery vehicles, lowering fuel consumption and emissions.

LAST-MILE DELIVERY

- **Electric and Hybrid Vehicles:** Last-mile delivery, particularly in urban areas, can be a significant source of emissions. Employing electric or hybrid vehicles for these short-distance deliveries reduces air pollution and noise in urban centres. Many cities are implementing regulations that encourage or require eco-friendly last-mile delivery options.

- **Route Optimisation:** Advanced route optimisation software can enhance the efficiency of last-mile delivery by identifying the most fuel-efficient routes, reducing delivery times, and minimising vehicle idling. Data-driven decision-making helps maximise delivery capacity while minimising the environmental impact.
- **Micro-Hubs and Urban Consolidation Centres:** Establishing micro-hubs or urban consolidation centres strategically placed within cities can reduce the number of delivery vehicles on the road. These centres consolidate deliveries, reducing the distance travelled by each vehicle and minimising congestion and emissions.

Sustainable warehousing and distribution practices are essential for reducing the logistics industry's ecological footprint. By adopting green warehouse initiatives and employing eco-friendly last-mile delivery methods, companies contribute to a cleaner environment and align with evolving regulations and customer expectations for sustainable logistics solutions.

10. COLLABORATION AND KNOWLEDGE SHARING:

Collaboration and knowledge sharing are fundamental in driving sustainability initiatives within the maritime industry. This section explores two key strategies: Stakeholder Collaboration and Engagement with Industry Associations.

STAKEHOLDER COLLABORATION

- **Cross-Industry Collaboration:** Maritime companies should actively engage with industry stakeholders, including shipping companies, port authorities, government agencies, and environmental organisations. By fostering collaboration, these stakeholders can share best practices, research findings, and innovative solutions for sustainability.
- **Data Sharing:** Collaboration also involves sharing critical data related to emissions, environmental impact assessments, and technological advancements. By exchanging data and insights, stakeholders can collectively identify areas for improvement and coordinate efforts to reduce the industry's environmental footprint.
- **Policy and Regulation:** Collaborating with government agencies is essential in shaping environmental policies and regulations. Industry stakeholders can work together to advocate for environmentally responsible legislation that promotes sustainable practices and incentivises eco-friendly investments.

ENGAGEMENT WITH INDUSTRY ASSOCIATIONS

- **Membership in Associations:** Maritime companies should actively participate in industry associations focusing on sustainable shipping practices. These associations, such as the International Chamber of Shipping (ICS) or the Global Maritime Forum, provide a platform for networking, knowledge exchange, and advocacy for sustainability.
- **Access to Resources:** Industry associations often offer access to valuable resources, including research reports, guidelines, and best practice recommendations. These

resources help companies stay informed about the latest developments and technologies in sustainable shipping.
- **Advocacy and Representation:** By joining industry associations, maritime companies can collectively advocate for policies and initiatives that support sustainability. These associations represent the industry's collective voice and can influence regulatory decisions and industry standards.

Collaboration and knowledge sharing are essential to the maritime industry's sustainability journey. By working with stakeholders and engaging with industry associations, companies can tap into a wealth of expertise and resources to drive positive change, reduce environmental impact, and ensure a more sustainable future for the industry.

Sustainable logistics practices in maritime shipping reduce the industry's environmental impact and contribute to cost savings and improved operational efficiency. By adopting these practices, the maritime sector can play a significant role in achieving global sustainability goals while ensuring the efficient movement of goods around the world.

EFFICIENCY IMPROVEMENTS ALONG THE SUPPLY CHAIN IN MARITIME SHIPPING

Efficiency improvements along the supply chain in maritime shipping are vital for reducing costs, enhancing competitiveness, and minimising the industry's environmental footprint. Here are key areas where efficiency enhancements can be implemented:

1. Inventory Management:

Effective inventory management is a pivotal aspect of streamlined operations within any industry, and the maritime sector is no exception. In this context, two fundamental strategies, Demand Forecasting and Just-in-Time (JIT) Inventory practices, stand as keystones in achieving efficiency and cost reduction.

DEMAND FORECASTING

Accurate demand forecasting is the compass guiding inventory management in maritime shipping. Leveraging advanced forecasting tools and data analytics, companies can precisely anticipate demand patterns. Doing so ensures that they procure and stock the right quantities of goods, avoiding the costly pitfalls of excess inventory. Not only does this strategy lead to cost savings in terms of storage, but it also minimises the risk of goods becoming obsolete or deteriorating in storage. The environmental benefits are also significant, as reduced inventory levels equate to lower energy consumption and emissions associated with storage facilities.

JUST-IN-TIME (JIT) INVENTORY

JIT inventory practices are the embodiment of efficiency and cost-consciousness in maritime logistics. The core principle is ensuring that goods arrive precisely when needed, leaving minimal room for warehousing excesses. By synchronising inventory levels with actual demand, companies can significantly reduce warehousing requirements, translating to substantial cost reductions. Additionally, the JIT approach aligns with sustainability goals by minimising the ecological footprint associated with warehousing operations. Fewer storage facilities mean less energy consumption, reduced maintenance, and a lighter environmental impact.

In essence, integrating Demand Forecasting and JIT Inventory practices in maritime inventory management is not merely about efficiency and cost savings; it's a commitment to environmental responsibility. By procuring, storing, and transporting goods with greater precision and reduced waste, the industry takes significant strides towards a more sustainable future while maintaining its competitiveness and operational excellence.

2. CARGO HANDLING AND STOWAGE

Efficient cargo handling and stowage practices are at the heart of maritime logistics, shaping not only the economics but also the sustainability of the industry. In this regard, two key strategies, Automated Handling and Optimal Stowage, shine as beacons of innovation and environmental responsibility.

AUTOMATED HANDLING

Adopting automated cargo handling systems at ports heralds a transformative era in maritime logistics. These advanced systems leverage robotics and smart technologies to streamline the loading and unloading of vessels. By significantly accelerating these processes, automated handling reduces vessel turnaround times to a minimum. This efficiency reduces fuel consumption and emissions, as vessels spend less time idling at ports. Moreover, automation's precise and consistent nature minimises the risk of accidents and mishandling, further enhancing safety and environmental stewardship.

OPTIMAL STOWAGE

The art of optimal stowage is elevated to science through computer algorithms and simulations. These technologies determine the perfect cargo arrangement on vessels, maximising space utilisation while adhering to safety and stability requirements. The result is an orchestra of efficiency, where every square inch of cargo space is optimised, minimising the need for additional voyages or larger vessels. At its core, this practice is a testament to sustainability, as it directly reduces transport costs and associated emissions. Furthermore, optimal stowage enhances vessel stability, reducing the risk of accidents and cargo damage.

The integration of Automated Handling and Optimal Stowage practices epitomises the maritime industry's dedication to both efficiency and sustainability. By accelerating cargo handling processes and optimising stowage, the industry reduces operational costs and curtails its environmental footprint. These advancements herald a new era of eco-conscious maritime logistics, where innovation and environmental responsibility coexist harmoniously.

3. PAPERLESS TRANSACTIONS:

The transition to paperless transactions within the maritime industry represents a significant leap forward regarding efficiency, accuracy, and sustainability. This shift is characterised by two pivotal strategies: Electronic Documentation and the incorporation of Blockchain Technology.

ELECTRONIC DOCUMENTATION

Embracing electronic documentation marks a transformative shift away from cumbersome paperwork and manual processes. By transitioning to electronic bills of lading, invoices, and customs declarations, the maritime industry can streamline its operations on multiple fronts.

Firstly, electronic documentation reduces the likelihood of errors and inaccuracies often associated with manual paperwork. This not only saves time but also reduces the risk of costly delays and disputes. Furthermore, electronic documentation expedites clearance processes at ports and customs, ensuring cargo flows smoothly through supply chains.

In addition to efficiency gains, the environmental benefits of electronic documentation are substantial. Reducing paper usage conserves natural resources and decreases waste, aligning with sustainability objectives. Moreover, electronic documentation significantly reduces the energy consumption and carbon emissions associated with producing, transporting, and disposing of paper documents.

BLOCKCHAIN TECHNOLOGY

Blockchain technology has emerged as a potent force in revolutionising the transparency, traceability, and security of transactions within the maritime industry. By implementing blockchain-based supply chain platforms, the industry can achieve a new level of trust and efficiency.

Blockchain ensures the immutability of transaction records, making them resistant to fraud and tampering. This level of security enhances the integrity of the supply chain, reducing the risk of fraudulent activities and disputes.

Furthermore, blockchain provides end-to-end visibility and traceability, allowing stakeholders to track the journey of goods in real time. This transparency reduces the likelihood of cargo theft and enables quick response to disruptions, such as spoilage or damage, which can lead to waste reduction and enhanced sustainability.

Adopting paperless transactions in maritime logistics is a pivotal step towards efficiency and sustainability. Electronic documentation minimises errors, expedites processes, and reduces waste, while blockchain technology enhances trust, security, and traceability. These advancements signify a maritime industry that is technologically advanced and dedicated to eco-conscious practices.

4. TRANSPORT MODES INTEGRATION:

Integrating various transport modes is a strategic approach that can greatly enhance maritime logistics' efficiency and sustainability. In this context, two key strategies, Intermodal Transport and Transshipment Hubs, play pivotal roles in creating seamless supply chains and reducing environmental impact.

INTERMODAL TRANSPORT

Intermodal transport is the linchpin of a multi-modal approach to shipping that combines sea, rail, and road transport to create efficient, integrated supply chains. This approach offers several key advantages:

- **Minimised Transit Times:** By seamlessly transitioning cargo between different modes of transport, intermodal systems can significantly reduce transit times. This enhances efficiency and reduces the environmental impact associated with prolonged journeys and excessive fuel consumption.
- **Emissions Reduction:** Intermodal transport minimises the reliance on long-haul trucking, which tends to be more carbon-intensive. Instead, it leverages the energy efficiency of sea transport for long-distance journeys and supplements it with rail or road for shorter distances. This reduces overall emissions and contributes to sustainability goals.
- **Cargo Flexibility:** Intermodal systems offer greater flexibility in cargo handling. Different modes of transport can be selected based on cargo size, urgency, and destination, optimising routes for economic and environmental efficiency.

TRANSSHIPMENT HUBS

Transhipment hubs are strategically located facilities that facilitate cargo transfer between vessels efficiently. These hubs serve as central points where goods are loaded from smaller vessels onto larger ones or vice versa. The benefits of transshipment hubs include:

- Route Optimisation: Transshipment hubs enable vessels to follow more direct routes, reducing the need to visit multiple smaller ports. This results in shorter voyages, translating into lower fuel consumption, reduced emissions, and minimised operational costs.
- Economies of Scale: By consolidating cargo at transhipment hubs, larger vessels can be utilised for long-haul routes. These larger vessels are often more energy-efficient per cargo unit, reducing emissions per ton-kilometre.
- Efficient Cargo Handling: Transshipment hubs have advanced cargo handling equipment and systems, ensuring that cargo transfer is swift and seamless. This efficiency reduces vessel turnaround times and enhances the overall supply chain performance.

Integrating transport modes through intermodal transport and establishing transhipment hubs are pivotal strategies in the maritime industry's quest for sustainability. These approaches optimise routes, reduce emissions, enhance efficiency and reinforce the industry's commitment to responsible logistics practices.

5. DATA ANALYTICS AND VISIBILITY:

Integrating data analytics and enhanced visibility practices is ushering in a new era of efficiency, resilience, and sustainability within the maritime industry. This section explores two pivotal strategies: Real-time Monitoring and Predictive Analytics.

REAL-TIME MONITORING

Real-time monitoring through IoT sensors and data analytics revolutionises cargo tracking and supply chain management. This approach brings several notable benefits:

- Proactive Issue Resolution: Real-time monitoring enables stakeholders to track cargo movements, temperature, humidity, and other crucial parameters in real time. This real-time visibility allows for rapidly identifying issues like deviations from planned routes or adverse environmental conditions. With this information, proactive measures can be taken to resolve problems promptly, minimising cargo damage and disruption risk.
- Enhanced Visibility: Real-time monitoring provides stakeholders with an unprecedented level of visibility throughout the supply chain. This transparency extends to cargo conditions, location, and estimated arrival time, empowering stakeholders to make informed decisions, optimise operations, and respond swiftly to changes or disruptions.
- Resource Optimisation: The data generated by real-time monitoring can be leveraged to optimise resource allocation. For example, if it's known that a particular cargo is delayed, other resources can be redirected to address the issue or prioritise the delivery of other goods. This resource optimisation enhances efficiency and contributes to sustainability by reducing waste and energy consumption.

PREDICTIVE ANALYTICS

Predictive analytics takes data-driven decision-making to the next level by using historical data and real-time information to anticipate supply chain disruptions. This practice offers several key advantages:

- Disruption Mitigation: Predictive analytics can forecast potential disruptions, such as adverse weather events, labour strikes, or port congestion. Armed with this information, companies can proactively adjust their routing, scheduling, and resource allocation to mitigate the impact of disruptions, reducing delays and costs.
- Optimised Routing: By analysing historical data and real-time information, predictive analytics can determine the most efficient routes for cargo transport. This optimisation minimises fuel consumption and emissions, contributing to environmental sustainability.
- Resource Allocation: Predictive analytics can assist in allocating resources such as vessels, trucks, and personnel. This ensures that resources are deployed where they are most needed, optimising operational efficiency and reducing waste.

Integrating real-time monitoring and predictive analytics is a game-changer for the maritime industry. These strategies enhance visibility and responsiveness, improve resource allocation, reduce disruptions, and contribute to environmental sustainability by optimising operations and reducing waste.

6. ENERGY-EFFICIENT TRANSPORTATION:

Embracing energy-efficient transportation practices is a cornerstone of the maritime industry's sustainability efforts. This strategic approach entails two key components: adopting Eco-Friendly Vehicles and implementing Route Optimisation measures.

ECO-FRIENDLY VEHICLES

Investing in fuel-efficient and low-emission vehicles for the inland movement of goods is a pivotal step towards reducing the industry's environmental footprint. By opting for vehicles powered by alternative fuels, such as liquefied natural gas (LNG) or electricity, maritime companies can significantly lower their carbon emissions and decrease their reliance on fossil fuels. These eco-friendly vehicles contribute to a cleaner environment and align with increasingly stringent emissions regulations, positioning companies as responsible stewards of the environment. Furthermore, adopting these vehicles signals a commitment to sustainability that resonates with eco-conscious customers and stakeholders, bolstering a company's reputation and competitiveness.

ROUTE OPTIMISATION

Route optimisation is a dynamic strategy that leverages data and technology to select the most fuel-efficient and congestion-free transport routes. By utilising route optimisation software, maritime companies can make informed decisions that minimise fuel consumption and emissions. These software solutions factor in many variables, including traffic conditions, road quality, and even weather patterns, to determine the optimal routes for cargo transportation. The result is a reduction in operational costs and a notable decrease in the ecological footprint associated with each journey. In essence, route optimisation is about cost savings and contributing to a greener, more sustainable industry.

Energy-efficient transportation practices represent a crucial pillar in the maritime industry's commitment to sustainability. By adopting eco-friendly vehicles and route optimisation, the industry reduces its environmental impact, lowers operational costs, and positions itself as a responsible leader in eco-conscious logistics. These practices benefit the bottom line and contribute to a healthier planet and a more resilient and competitive maritime sector.

7. PORT EFFICIENCY:

Port efficiency is a linchpin of maritime logistics, and the integration of advanced technologies is steering the industry toward unprecedented efficiency and sustainability. This section focuses on two vital strategies: Smart Ports and Port Automation.

SMART PORTS

Implementing smart port technologies is revolutionising every facet of port operations, from vessel berthing to cargo handling and port logistics. Smart ports leverage diverse cutting-edge solutions, including the Internet of Things (IoT), data analytics, and real-time monitoring, to optimise operations and enhance efficiency. These technologies offer several key benefits:

- **Efficient Vessel Berthing:** Smart port technologies provide real-time data on vessel positions, enabling precise and efficient berthing. Vessels can be accurately scheduled for arrival and departure, reducing idle times and enhancing overall port throughput.
- **Cargo Handling Optimisation:** Smart ports enable tracking cargo movements, both within the port and throughout the supply chain. This real-time visibility ensures that cargo is handled efficiently, reducing dwell times and minimising the risk of damage or theft.
- **Logistics Efficiency:** Smart port technologies extend their benefits to logistics operations, enabling the seamless coordination of cargo movements with hinterland transportation networks. This ensures that cargo flows smoothly from the port to the final destination, minimising congestion and emissions associated with transportation.

PORT AUTOMATION

Incorporating automation in port operations is another significant driver of efficiency and sustainability. Port automation involves the deployment of autonomous cranes, container handling equipment, and other machinery to streamline cargo handling. The advantages of port automation are manifold:

- **Labor Cost Reduction:** Automation reduces the need for manual labour in port operations, leading to cost savings for port authorities and operators. This allows resources to be allocated more efficiently, enhancing overall financial sustainability.
- **Consistency and Precision:** Automated systems operate with remarkable consistency and precision, minimising the risk of human error. This consistency enhances safety and reduces the likelihood of accidents, damage to cargo, or operational disruptions.
- **Energy Efficiency:** Automated equipment is often designed to be more energy-efficient than their manual counterparts. They can optimise energy consumption by adjusting their operations based on real-time data, further contributing to sustainability efforts.

The adoption of smart port technologies and port automation represents a paradigm shift in the maritime industry's pursuit of efficiency and sustainability. These strategies improve port throughput and reduce costs, enhance safety, reduce emissions, and position the industry as a pioneer in eco-conscious logistics.

8. SUSTAINABLE WAREHOUSING:

Sustainable warehousing practices are pivotal in reducing the ecological footprint of the maritime logistics industry. This section emphasises two fundamental strategies: Energy-Efficient Facilities and Automated Storage and Retrieval Systems.

ENERGY-EFFICIENT FACILITIES

The design and operation of energy-efficient warehouses represent a cornerstone of sustainability within the maritime industry. These facilities are characterised by several key attributes:

- **Advanced Lighting Solutions:** Energy-efficient warehouses leverage advanced lighting systems, such as LED lighting, that consume significantly less energy than traditional lighting options. These systems reduce electricity bills and contribute to sustainability by curbing energy consumption and emissions.
- **Optimised Heating and Cooling:** Energy-efficient warehouses have state-of-the-art heating and cooling systems to minimise energy use. These systems often incorporate smart thermostats and sensors that adjust temperature settings based on occupancy and environmental conditions, further reducing energy waste.
- **Solar Power Integration:** Many sustainable warehouses integrate renewable energy sources like solar panels to generate clean electricity on-site. This reduces reliance on fossil fuels and helps warehouses operate more sustainably by reducing their carbon footprint.

By embracing energy-efficient facility design and operation, the maritime industry lowers operational costs and advances its commitment to environmental sustainability.

AUTOMATED STORAGE AND RETRIEVAL SYSTEMS

Implementing automated storage and retrieval systems is a pivotal step toward increasing warehouse efficiency while minimising manual labour. These systems bring multiple advantages:

- **Labor Reduction:** Automated systems significantly reduce the need for manual labour in warehousing operations. This lowers labour costs, enhances worker safety, and reduces the industry's reliance on labour-intensive practices.
- **Optimised Space Utilisation:** Automated storage and retrieval systems are designed to maximise warehouse space utilisation. They can stack and retrieve goods precisely, optimising storage capacity, minimising the need for larger warehouses, and reducing associated construction and operational costs.
- **Energy Efficiency:** Automated systems are often engineered for energy efficiency. They can operate with high precision, minimising unnecessary movements and energy consumption. This energy-conscious approach aligns with sustainability goals and reduces the environmental impact of warehousing operations.

Sustainable warehousing practices are a pivotal component of the maritime industry's commitment to eco-conscious logistics. Through the adoption of energy-efficient facilities and the implementation of automated storage and retrieval systems, the industry enhances efficiency, reduces operational costs, and contributes to a greener, more sustainable future. These practices represent a smart business strategy and a responsible environmental stewardship commitment.

9. REVERSE LOGISTICS:

Reverse logistics is an increasingly important aspect of sustainable supply chain management, and it encompasses two critical strategies: Product Returns Optimisation and Remanufacturing.

PRODUCT RETURNS OPTIMISATION

Efficiently handling product returns is essential for reducing waste and minimising associated costs within the maritime logistics industry. This involves the development of streamlined processes and sustainable practices:

- Recycling and Repurposing: Implementing efficient processes for recycling or repurposing returned products can significantly reduce waste. By segregating returned items into categories suitable for recycling or repurposing, the industry can maximise resource recovery and minimise landfill waste. This not only aligns with environmental sustainability but also reduces disposal costs.
- Reducing Transportation Impact: Reverse logistics often involves transporting returned goods. Optimising transportation routes and load factors minimises fuel consumption and emissions. Consolidating returns and utilising efficient transportation methods contribute to sustainability while controlling operational expenses.
- Minimising Return Rates: While not directly related to reverse logistics, the industry can also work to minimise product return rates through improved quality control and customer support. This proactive approach reduces the need for reverse logistics processes in the first place, benefiting both the environment and cost management.

REMANUFACTURING

Remanufacturing is a strategy that extends the lifecycle of returned products and reduces the need for new production. It involves the following practices:

- **Refurbishing Returned Products:** Instead of discarding returned products, maritime companies can explore opportunities to refurbish them to like-new condition. This practice not only reduces waste but also conserves materials and energy that would be required for manufacturing new products.
- **Extending Product Lifecycles:** Remanufacturing prolongs the useful life of products, contributing to sustainability goals by reducing the demand for new resources and minimising waste. It aligns with the principles of the circular economy, where products are designed to be reused and remanufactured rather than disposed of after a single use.
- **Economic and Environmental Benefits:** Remanufactured products often offer cost savings for customers, making them an attractive option. Additionally, the reduced environmental impact associated with remanufacturing supports an eco-friendlier image for maritime companies.

When approached with strategies like Product Returns Optimisation and Remanufacturing, reverse logistics reduces waste and costs and promotes environmental sustainability. These practices align with the principles of the circular economy, reduce the industry's ecological footprint, and contribute to a more resource-efficient and responsible maritime logistics sector.

10. COLLABORATION AND VISIBILITY:

Collaboration and enhanced visibility are at the forefront of modern supply chain management within the maritime industry. This section underscores two fundamental strategies: Supply Chain Collaboration and establishing Supply Chain Control Towers.

SUPPLY CHAIN COLLABORATION

Collaboration among supply chain partners is a linchpin of efficiency and sustainability within the maritime sector. This strategy brings together various stakeholders, including shipping companies, port authorities, logistics providers, and manufacturers, to collectively optimise processes and operations:

- Data Sharing and Insights: Collaborative efforts involve sharing critical data and insights among supply chain partners. This data exchange enhances visibility throughout the supply chain, enabling stakeholders to make informed decisions, streamline operations, and respond promptly to changes or disruptions.
- Risk Mitigation: By pooling resources and knowledge, supply chain collaboration helps mitigate risk. Partners can collectively identify potential bottlenecks, vulnerabilities, and disruptions, allowing for proactive planning and strategies to minimise the impact of unforeseen events.
- Efficiency Gains: Collaboration streamlines processes and eliminates redundancies. It optimises the allocation of resources and promotes the use of best practices, ultimately reducing costs and enhancing overall supply chain efficiency.

SUPPLY CHAIN CONTROL TOWERS

Establishing supply chain control towers represents a visionary approach to real-time monitoring and decision-making. These control towers serve as nerve centres that provide end-to-end visibility and coordination across the supply chain:

- **Real-Time Monitoring:** Supply chain control towers leverage advanced technologies such as IoT sensors, data analytics, and AI to monitor cargo movements, transportation conditions, and logistics operations in real time. This visibility enables stakeholders to proactively address issues, reduce delays, and enhance supply chain performance.
- **Predictive Analytics:** Control towers often incorporate predictive analytics to anticipate potential disruptions. By analysing historical data and real-time information, they can forecast disruptions, optimise routing, and allocate resources effectively, reducing the impact of unexpected events.
- **Streamlined Decision-Making:** Control towers facilitate rapid decision-making by providing stakeholders with a real-time view of the supply chain. This ensures that decisions are data-driven and aligned with sustainability and efficiency objectives.

Collaboration and visibility are integral to the maritime industry's sustainability and operational excellence quest. Through Supply Chain Collaboration and implementing Supply Chain Control Towers, stakeholders work together to optimise processes, enhance visibility, and respond effectively to challenges. These strategies reduce costs and promote environmental sustainability by minimising waste and emissions throughout the supply chain.

Efficiency improvements along the supply chain in maritime shipping contribute to cost reduction, environmental sustainability, and enhanced competitiveness in the global marketplace. By adopting these practices and continually optimising operations, the industry can achieve greater efficiency and reduce its carbon footprint.

TECHNOLOGY-ENABLED SOLUTIONS FOR GREENER OPERATIONS IN MARITIME SHIPPING

Technology plays a pivotal role in enabling greener and more sustainable operations in maritime shipping. Here are key technology-enabled solutions that contribute to eco-friendly practices in the industry:

1. SMART SHIPPING AND NAVIGATION SYSTEMS:

Smart shipping and navigation systems are ushering in a new era of safety, efficiency, and sustainability within the maritime industry. These technologies represent a quantum leap forward in vessel operations and environmental responsibility.

E-NAVIGATION

Implementing electronic navigation systems, known as E-Navigation, is transforming how vessels navigate the world's oceans. E-Navigation equips vessels with real-time access to critical data, including up-to-the-minute weather information, route optimisation suggestions, and details about shipping lanes. By leveraging this data, vessels can make informed decisions on their routes, choosing the most fuel-efficient paths that minimise exposure to adverse weather conditions. This optimisation enhances fuel efficiency and reduces emissions, aligning with the industry's sustainability goals. Additionally, E-Navigation contributes to safety by providing timely information about potential hazards, allowing vessels to take proactive measures to avoid accidents and environmental disasters.

AIS (AUTOMATIC IDENTIFICATION SYSTEM)

The Automatic Identification System (AIS) plays a pivotal role in enhancing vessel tracking and collision avoidance. By equipping vessels with AIS transponders, maritime authorities, other vessels, and coastal stations can continuously monitor their positions and movements. This real-time tracking reduces the risk of collisions and enhances overall safety at sea. AIS also serves as a vital tool for search and rescue operations, contributing to maritime security and disaster response. By mitigating the risk of accidents, AIS indirectly reduces the potential for oil spills and other environmental disasters, protecting fragile marine ecosystems.

Smart shipping and navigation systems are a beacon of progress in the maritime industry, blending safety, efficiency, and environmental responsibility. Adopting E-Navigation and AIS technology optimises routes, enhances safety, and directly contributes to sustainability efforts by reducing fuel consumption, emissions, and the risk of environmental disasters. These technologies represent a transformative shift toward a more resilient and eco-conscious maritime sector.

2. ALTERNATIVE FUELS AND ENERGY-EFFICIENT PROPULSION:

Alternative fuels and energy-efficient propulsion systems are at the forefront of the maritime industry's commitment to reducing its environmental impact. These innovative technologies are key to significantly reducing greenhouse gas emissions and fuel consumption.

LNG-POWERED VESSELS

Investing in LNG-powered ships represents a pivotal step toward a more sustainable maritime industry. LNG, or liquefied natural gas, is a cleaner-burning fuel compared to traditional bunker fuels. LNG-powered vessels emit significantly fewer greenhouse gases, sulphur oxides, and particulate matter, making them a more environmentally responsible choice. By adopting LNG propulsion, maritime companies reduce their carbon footprint and adhere to increasingly stringent emissions regulations. This transition to cleaner fuels aligns with global efforts to combat climate change and positions the industry as a responsible steward of the environment.

HYBRID AND BATTERY TECHNOLOGY

Developing hybrid vessels and battery-electric propulsion systems is another promising avenue for reducing emissions and fuel consumption. These innovative technologies offer several notable advantages:

Hybrid vessels combine traditional propulsion systems with electric power sources, allowing greater flexibility and efficiency. They can switch between power sources based on operational needs, optimising fuel consumption and emissions. On the other hand, battery-electric propulsion systems rely entirely on electricity, reducing or eliminating the need for fossil fuels. These systems are particularly well-suited for short-distance and port operations, contributing to cleaner air in coastal areas.

By investing in hybrid and battery technology, maritime companies reduce their environmental impact and enhance operational efficiency. These technologies align with sustainability goals and position the industry as a pioneer in clean energy adoption.

The maritime industry's embrace of alternative fuels and energy-efficient propulsion systems is a transformative shift toward a greener, more sustainable future. The adoption of LNG-powered vessels and the development of hybrid and battery technology represent a commitment to reducing emissions, conserving resources, and protecting the environment. These innovations position the industry as a leader in responsible energy use and environmental stewardship.

3. RENEWABLE ENERGY INTEGRATION:

Renewable energy integration in maritime operations marks a pivotal shift toward eco-conscious and sustainable practices. This section emphasises two key strategies: Wind-Assisted Propulsion and Solar Panels.

WIND-ASSISTED PROPULSION

The incorporation of wind-assisted propulsion systems, such as sails and rotors, heralds a renaissance in harnessing wind energy for maritime use. These systems offer numerous advantages:

- **Fuel Savings:** Wind-assisted propulsion reduces the reliance on fossil fuels by utilising wind energy to propel vessels. This translates into significant fuel savings and a marked reduction in greenhouse gas emissions. As the sails or rotors capture the power of the wind, vessels can reduce engine usage, especially during favourable wind conditions.
- **Environmental Stewardship:** Wind-assisted propulsion aligns with global efforts to combat climate change and reduce the maritime industry's carbon footprint. By tapping into a renewable energy source, vessels contribute to cleaner air and reduce pollution in coastal areas and beyond.
- **Cost Efficiency:** Over the long term, wind-assisted propulsion can lead to cost savings through reduced fuel consumption. While initial investments may be required for system installation and maintenance, the operational benefits, including lower fuel costs and emissions, make these systems economically attractive.

SOLAR PANELS

Installing solar panels on ship decks is another innovative strategy for sustainably generating onboard electricity. Solar panels offer several key benefits:

- **Clean Energy Generation:** Solar panels convert sunlight into electricity, providing a clean and renewable power source for onboard systems and equipment. This reduces the need for conventional power sources, such as generators, which rely on fossil fuels.
- **Reduced Fuel Consumption:** Solar panels reduce the vessel's reliance on traditional power generation methods, such as diesel generators. This results in lower fuel consumption and emissions, aligning with sustainability objectives.
- **Energy Independence:** Solar panels offer a degree of energy independence by generating power while the vessel is at sea or docked. This can enhance operational flexibility and reduce costs associated with onboard power generation.

Renewable energy integration in maritime operations through wind-assisted propulsion and solar panels represents a promising path toward a more sustainable industry. These strategies reduce fuel consumption and emissions and align with global efforts to transition to cleaner and more responsible energy sources. By harnessing the power of wind and sunlight, the maritime sector is charting a course toward a more eco-conscious and resilient future.

4. EMISSION CONTROL TECHNOLOGIES:

Emission control technologies are pivotal in mitigating the environmental impact of maritime operations while ensuring compliance with international regulations. This section emphasises two key strategies: Scrubbers and Selective Catalytic Reduction (SCR) systems.

SCRUBBERS

Installing exhaust gas cleaning systems, commonly known as scrubbers, represents a proactive approach to reducing sulphur oxide emissions from maritime vessels. These systems offer several significant advantages:

- **Sulphur Emissions Reduction:** Scrubbers remove sulphur dioxide (SO_2) from exhaust gases, effectively reducing sulphur oxide emissions. This is essential for compliance with international regulations, such as the International Maritime Organisation's (IMO) sulphur cap requirements.
- **Regulatory Compliance:** Scrubbers enable vessels to meet stringent emissions regulations without switching to low-sulphur fuels. This flexibility is particularly valuable for vessels operating in areas with limited low-sulphur fuel availability.
- **Fuel Cost Savings:** By using more affordable high-sulphur fuels while employing scrubbers, vessel operators can save fuel expenses, contributing to operational efficiency.

SELECTIVE CATALYTIC REDUCTION (SCR) SYSTEMS:

Selective Catalytic Reduction (SCR) systems are another crucial technology for reducing emissions from maritime vessels, specifically nitrogen oxide (NOx) emissions. These systems offer several key benefits:

- **NOx Emissions Reduction:** SCR systems convert NOx emissions into harmless nitrogen and water vapour through a chemical reaction. This results in a significant reduction in harmful NOx emissions, helping vessels meet emissions standards.
- **Environmental Impact:** By reducing NOx emissions, SCR systems contribute to improved air quality in coastal areas and sensitive ecosystems. This aligns with the industry's commitment to environmental responsibility.
- **Regulatory Compliance:** SCR systems are a valuable tool for compliance with emissions regulations, which are becoming increasingly stringent. Meeting these standards is legally required and vital for preserving the industry's reputation and ensuring sustainable operations.

Emission control technologies, such as scrubbers and SCR systems, are pivotal in reducing the environmental impact of maritime operations and ensuring compliance with international regulations. These technologies represent a commitment to cleaner air, reduced emissions, and a more sustainable future for the maritime industry.

5. IOT AND DATA ANALYTICS:

Integrating IoT (Internet of Things) and data analytics in maritime operations is ushering in a new era of efficiency, safety, and sustainability. This section highlights two key strategies: Sensor Networks and Predictive Analytics.

SENSOR NETWORKS

Deploying IoT sensors throughout vessels and cargo holds represents a transformative shift in monitoring and maintaining maritime assets. These sensor networks offer several significant advantages:

- **Real-Time Monitoring:** IoT sensors continuously collect data on various conditions, such as temperature, humidity, and equipment performance. This real-time monitoring ensures that any anomalies or deviations from desired parameters can be identified promptly, allowing for proactive maintenance and issue resolution.
- **Cargo Optimisation:** IoT sensors provide critical insights into cargo conditions, ensuring that goods are stored and transported optimally. This minimises the risk of damage and reduces waste, benefiting operational efficiency and sustainability.
- **Energy Efficiency:** Sensors also play a crucial role in optimising fuel consumption by providing data on engine performance and operational parameters. This data can be used to adjust vessel operations in real-time, reducing fuel waste and emissions.

PREDICTIVE ANALYTICS

The use of data analytics, particularly predictive analytics, is transforming maritime decision-making by leveraging historical data to anticipate future events and optimise operations:

- Equipment Maintenance: Predictive analytics can forecast equipment failures based on historical performance data. This proactive approach allows for timely maintenance and repairs, reducing downtime and improving operational efficiency. It also prevents potential accidents or environmental incidents caused by equipment failures.
- Fuel Consumption Optimisation: By analysing historical data on fuel consumption, predictive analytics can identify patterns and trends. This information can optimise fuel usage by adjusting vessel speed, route planning, and other operational parameters.
- Route Planning and Optimisation: Predictive analytics can forecast weather conditions, traffic patterns, and other factors that impact route planning. This information enables vessels to choose the most efficient and environmentally responsible routes, reducing fuel consumption and emissions.

Integrating IoT sensor networks and predictive analytics is a game-changer for the maritime industry. These technologies enhance operational efficiency and safety and contribute to sustainability by optimising resource utilisation, reducing emissions, and minimising waste. They position the industry as a pioneer in data-driven, eco-conscious logistics practices.

6. ENERGY MANAGEMENT SYSTEMS:

Energy management systems are pivotal in the maritime industry's quest for sustainability and operational efficiency. This section underscores two vital strategies: Energy Efficiency Monitoring and Load Management.

ENERGY EFFICIENCY MONITORING

Implementing energy management systems for monitoring and controlling energy consumption within ships represents a proactive approach to resource optimisation. These systems offer several significant advantages:

- **Real-Time Monitoring:** Energy management systems continuously monitor energy consumption across shipboard systems, lighting, and climate control. Real-time data allows immediate insights into energy usage patterns and anomalies, facilitating proactive energy-saving measures.
- **Efficient Resource Allocation:** By analysing energy consumption data, these systems help optimise resource allocation. Lighting, HVAC systems, and other shipboard equipment can be fine-tuned to operate more efficiently, reducing energy waste and operational costs.
- **Environmental Responsibility:** Energy efficiency monitoring aligns with the maritime industry's commitment to environmental responsibility. By reducing energy consumption, vessels can lower their carbon footprint and minimise their impact on fragile marine ecosystems.

LOAD MANAGEMENT

Load management is a strategy that focuses on optimising the distribution of power on board vessels. This practice reduces energy waste and ensures the efficient use of generators. Key benefits include:

- **Resource Optimisation:** Load management systems ensure power is distributed efficiently based on operational needs. This prevents overloading generators and minimises energy waste, contributing to operational efficiency.
- **Fuel Savings:** By reducing the need for excess power generation, load management directly translates into fuel savings. This not only reduces operational costs but also lowers emissions, aligning with sustainability goals.
- **Extended Equipment Lifespan:** By preventing power surges and overloads, load management systems extend the lifespan of shipboard equipment and systems. This reduces maintenance and replacement costs while enhancing the vessel's overall reliability.

Energy management systems encompassing energy efficiency monitoring and load management represent a significant stride toward a more sustainable and efficient maritime industry. These technologies optimise energy use, reduce operational costs, and align with environmental responsibility, positioning the industry as a responsible steward of resources and a pioneer in eco-conscious logistics practices.

7. BLOCKCHAIN AND TRANSPARENCY:

Blockchain technology is ushering in a new era of transparency and accountability in maritime logistics. This section emphasises two pivotal strategies: Supply Chain Transparency and Emission Tracking.

SUPPLY CHAIN TRANSPARENCY

Using blockchain technology to establish transparent and traceable supply chains is a transformative shift within the maritime industry. This strategy offers several significant advantages:

- **Sustainable Sourcing:** Blockchain technology enables the creation of immutable records that document the origin and journey of materials and products. This transparency ensures that sourcing practices align with sustainability goals, preventing using unethical or environmentally harmful sources.
- **Traceability:** With blockchain, stakeholders can trace the entire lifecycle of products, from raw materials to final delivery. This traceability is invaluable for verifying the authenticity of goods, ensuring compliance with regulations, and responding promptly to issues such as product recalls or contamination.
- **Consumer Confidence:** Transparent supply chains instil consumer confidence by providing visibility into the origins and sustainability of products. Consumers increasingly seek ethically and sustainably sourced goods, and blockchain technology helps meet these demands.

EMISSION TRACKING

Recording and verifying emissions data on a blockchain is a powerful strategy for tracking and reducing emissions along the maritime supply chain. Key benefits include:

- **Real-Time Data:** Blockchain enables the real-time recording and verification of emissions data from vessels and transportation processes. This data provides stakeholders immediate insights into emissions levels, facilitating proactive emission reduction measures.
- **Compliance Assurance:** Emission tracking on blockchain ensures compliance with international emissions regulations. It offers an immutable record of emissions, making it easier to demonstrate adherence to standards and regulations.
- **Emission Reduction:** By providing transparent emissions data, blockchain technology encourages stakeholders to reduce emissions actively. This includes optimising vessel operations, adopting cleaner fuels, and implementing efficiency measures throughout the supply chain.

Blockchain technology is a game-changer for transparency and sustainability within the maritime industry. Through strategies like Supply Chain Transparency and Emission Tracking, blockchain enhances accountability, promotes responsible sourcing, and reduces emissions. These technologies make the industry a leader in eco-conscious logistics and responsible supply chain management.

8. AUTONOMOUS AND REMOTE OPERATIONS:

Integrating autonomous and remote operations represents a transformative leap in maritime logistics, enhancing efficiency, safety, and sustainability. This section underscores two critical strategies: Remote Monitoring and Autonomous Shipping.

REMOTE MONITORING

Remote monitoring enables real-time oversight and control of vessel systems from a distance, reducing the need for physical presence on board. This strategy offers several noteworthy benefits:

- **Operational Efficiency:** Remote monitoring streamlines vessel operations by providing continuous access to critical data and system controls. Operators can make immediate adjustments to optimise performance, reducing fuel consumption and operational costs.
- **Safety:** Remote monitoring enhances safety by allowing operators to respond promptly to emergencies or system failures. It also reduces the need for personnel to be physically present in potentially hazardous environments.
- **Environmental Responsibility:** By optimising vessel operations through remote monitoring, maritime companies can reduce fuel consumption and emissions. This aligns with sustainability objectives and contributes to the industry's commitment to eco-conscious practices.

AUTONOMOUS SHIPPING

Developing autonomous vessels that can operate efficiently and make real-time decisions is a pioneering step toward a more sustainable maritime industry. Key benefits include:

- **Route Optimisation:** Autonomous vessels can analyse vast amounts of data, including weather conditions, traffic patterns, and cargo requirements, to optimise real-time routes. This reduces fuel consumption, emissions, and voyage durations.
- **Reduced Human Error:** Autonomous shipping minimises the potential for human error, which can lead to accidents, emissions, and inefficiencies. These systems rely on data-driven decision-making, enhancing operational safety and reliability.
- **Labor Efficiency:** Autonomous vessels require fewer onboard crew members, reducing operational costs associated with salaries, accommodations, and provisions. This leads to cost savings while improving overall efficiency.

Autonomous and remote operations are poised to revolutionise the maritime industry, making it more efficient, safer, and environmentally responsible. Through strategies like Remote Monitoring and Autonomous Shipping, the industry leverages advanced technologies to optimise operations, reduce emissions, and enhance sustainability. These innovations position maritime logistics at the forefront of responsible and forward-thinking transportation practices.

9. WASTE MANAGEMENT AND RECYCLING:

Waste management and recycling are integral components of sustainable maritime operations, addressing both environmental concerns and resource conservation. This section underscores two key strategies: Onboard Recycling Systems and Waste-to-Energy technologies.

ONBOARD RECYCLING SYSTEMS

Installing onboard recycling systems is a proactive approach to processing waste and minimising the environmental impact of disposal at sea. These systems offer several significant advantages:

- **Waste Reduction:** Onboard recycling systems enable the separation and processing of recyclable materials, reducing the volume of waste that must be disposed of at sea. This contributes to cleaner oceans and coastal areas.
- **Resource Conservation:** Recycling onboard vessels conserves valuable resources by repurposing plastics, glass, and paper. It reduces the demand for new raw materials and aligns with sustainability goals.
- **Environmental Responsibility:** By managing waste responsibly, maritime companies demonstrate a commitment to environmental responsibility and play a role in protecting marine ecosystems.

WASTE-TO-ENERGY

Exploring waste-to-energy technologies represents a cutting-edge strategy for converting waste into usable energy, reducing the need for additional power generation. Key benefits include:

- Energy Generation: Waste-to-energy technologies convert waste materials into electricity or thermal energy. This energy can power onboard systems and reduce the vessel's reliance on traditional power generation methods, such as diesel generators.
- Waste Reduction: Waste-to-energy systems reduce the volume of waste that needs to be stored or disposed of at sea. This minimises waste management costs and environmental impact.
- Operational Efficiency: By generating energy from waste materials, vessels can operate more efficiently and reduce fuel consumption. This aligns with sustainability objectives and contributes to cost savings.

Waste management and recycling practices are essential for maritime companies seeking to minimise their environmental footprint and operate sustainably. Strategies like Onboard Recycling Systems and Waste-to-Energy technologies reduce waste and resource consumption and demonstrate a commitment to responsible waste management and environmental stewardship. These initiatives position the maritime industry as a responsible and eco-conscious sector.

10. GREEN PORT TECHNOLOGIES:

Green port technologies are pivotal in reducing the environmental impact of port operations while enhancing sustainability and efficiency. This section highlights two crucial strategies: Shore Power Infrastructure and Sustainable Cargo Handling.

SHORE POWER INFRASTRUCTURE

Installing shore power facilities at ports is a groundbreaking strategy that allows vessels to connect to clean electricity while berthed. This approach offers several significant advantages:

- **Emissions Reduction:** Shore power infrastructure enables vessels to switch from onboard generators to clean, shore-based electricity while in port. This significantly reduces emissions, improving air quality in port areas and minimising the environmental impact of vessel operations.
- **Noise Reduction:** Shore power eliminates the noise pollution associated with onboard generators. This benefits the environment and the well-being of port workers and nearby communities.
- **Energy Efficiency:** Shore power is often sourced from renewable or lower-emission sources. By using cleaner electricity for various onboard systems and operations at the port, vessels reduce their carbon footprint and contribute to sustainability objectives.

SUSTAINABLE CARGO HANDLING

Investing in energy-efficient cargo handling equipment and automation represents a forward-thinking strategy to minimise energy consumption during loading and unloading processes. Key benefits include:

- **Operational Efficiency:** Energy-efficient cargo handling equipment and automation systems streamline port operations, reducing turnaround times and enhancing efficiency. This translates into cost savings and operational competitiveness.
- **Resource Conservation:** Automation and energy-efficient equipment minimise energy waste, contributing to reduced operational costs and a smaller environmental footprint. It also conserves energy resources, aligning with sustainability goals.
- **Environmental Responsibility:** Sustainable cargo handling practices are committed to environmental responsibility. By minimising energy consumption and emissions during port operations, maritime companies support a cleaner and more eco-conscious industry.

Green port technologies play a pivotal role in transforming the maritime industry into a more sustainable and efficient sector. Strategies like Shore Power Infrastructure and Sustainable Cargo Handling align with environmental responsibility, contribute to emissions reduction, and enhance the industry's reputation as a responsible steward of resources and a pioneer in eco-conscious logistics practices.

By embracing these technology-enabled solutions, maritime shipping can significantly reduce its environmental footprint, achieve greater operational efficiency, and transition toward a more sustainable and eco-friendly industry. These advancements benefit the environment and enhance the industry's long-term viability and competitiveness.

Chapter 12

ENERGY STORAGE AND MANAGEMENT

Energy storage and management are critical aspects of sustainable shipping, allowing vessels to optimise power generation and reduce environmental impact. This chapter delves into the importance of energy storage solutions, their integration with shipboard systems, and best practices for efficient energy management in the maritime industry.

THE IMPORTANCE OF ENERGY STORAGE IN RENEWABLE SHIPPING

Energy storage plays a pivotal role in advancing renewable shipping practices and achieving sustainability goals within the maritime industry. Here are key reasons why energy storage is crucial in renewable shipping:

1. SMOOTHING RENEWABLE ENERGY VARIABILITY:

Smoothing the variability of renewable energy sources is a fundamental challenge in transitioning toward a more sustainable and green energy landscape. This challenge arises from the intermittent nature of wind and solar power sources, where energy production fluctuates based on weather conditions and time of day. To address this variability, energy storage systems have emerged as a critical solution, bridging energy production and demand.

INTERMITTENT ENERGY SOURCES

Renewable energy sources, such as wind turbines and solar panels, offer numerous advantages, including reduced greenhouse gas emissions and a lower environmental footprint than fossil fuels. However, their intermittent nature presents operational challenges. These sources generate electricity when the wind blows or the sun shines, making energy production unpredictable. This intermittency can lead to periods of energy surplus and scarcity.

ENERGY STORAGE SYSTEMS

Energy storage systems, such as batteries and pumped hydro storage, play a pivotal role in mitigating the challenges of intermittent energy sources. These systems capture and store excess energy when production exceeds demand and release stored energy when production falls short. This buffering effect serves several essential functions:

- **Grid Stability:** Energy storage systems contribute to grid stability by balancing supply and demand. When renewable sources generate excess energy, it is stored for later use, ensuring a consistent and reliable energy supply even during periods of low production.

- **Peak Load Management:** Energy storage systems are particularly valuable during peak energy demand. They can discharge stored energy to meet high demand, reducing the need for conventional fossil-fuelled power plants often used during peak hours.
- **Energy Resilience:** Energy storage enhances energy resilience by providing backup power during grid outages or disruptions. This is crucial for critical infrastructure, businesses, and residential customers seeking uninterrupted power supply.
- **Renewable Integration:** Energy storage facilitates the integration of renewable energy into the grid. It allows utilities to maximise the use of renewable sources, even when weather conditions are unfavourable for energy production.

Energy storage systems are the linchpin in addressing the variability of intermittent renewable energy sources. They offer grid stability, enable efficient peak load management, enhance energy resilience, and foster the broader integration of renewable energy into the energy landscape. As technology advances and energy storage capacity grows, these systems will play a pivotal role in achieving a more sustainable and reliable energy future.

2. FUEL EFFICIENCY AND EMISSION REDUCTION:

Fuel efficiency and emission reduction are paramount concerns in the maritime industry as it seeks to transition toward more sustainable and environmentally responsible practices. The optimisation of propulsion through the use of energy storage systems represents a crucial strategy for achieving these objectives.

OPTIMISING PROPULSION

Traditionally, maritime vessels have relied heavily on conventional fossil fuels, such as diesel and heavy fuel oil, for propulsion. These fuels are associated with significant emissions of greenhouse gases (GHGs) and air pollutants, making them a major contributor to environmental degradation and climate change. However, the integration of energy storage systems allows vessels to embark on a more sustainable and eco-conscious journey:

- **Renewable Energy Utilisation:** Energy storage systems enable vessels to capture and store energy from renewable sources like wind and solar power. During favourable weather conditions, excess renewable energy is stored in batteries or other storage mediums. This stored energy can then be utilised for propulsion, reducing the vessel's reliance on traditional fossil fuels.
- **Reduced Emissions:** By harnessing renewable energy for propulsion, vessels can significantly reduce emissions of GHGs, sulphur oxides (SOx), nitrogen oxides (NOx), and particulate matter. This aligns with international emissions regulations and demonstrates a commitment to environmental responsibility.
- **Operational Efficiency:** Energy storage systems enhance the overall operational efficiency of vessels. They offer flexibility in power management, enabling vessels to optimise their energy use based on real-time conditions, including wind, solar, and sea conditions. This optimisation reduces fuel consumption and emissions.

- **Cost Savings:** Over the long term, adopting energy storage systems for propulsion can lead to substantial cost savings. While there may be initial investments in the technology, reduced fuel consumption and lower emissions-related expenses contribute to operational cost efficiency.

Optimising propulsion through integrating energy storage systems is a pivotal strategy for achieving fuel efficiency and emission reduction in the maritime industry. This approach reduces the sector's carbon footprint and aligns with global efforts to combat climate change and promote sustainability. It positions the maritime industry as a responsible and forward-thinking contributor to a more eco-conscious future.

3. ENHANCED OPERATIONAL FLEXIBILITY:

Enhanced operational flexibility, enabled by energy storage systems, is revolutionising the maritime industry by allowing vessels to adapt to diverse operational conditions efficiently and sustainably. This section emphasises the importance of dynamic power management in achieving this flexibility.

DYNAMIC POWER MANAGEMENT

Energy storage systems empower vessels to dynamically manage their power sources, seamlessly transitioning between renewable energy, battery power, and traditional fossil fuels as needed. This approach offers several key advantages:

- **Efficiency Optimisation:** Dynamic power management allows vessels to select the most efficient energy source based on real-time conditions. For instance, during favourable wind or solar energy production periods, the system can prioritise renewable sources to reduce fuel consumption and emissions. Conversely, when renewable energy availability is low, traditional fuels or battery power can take over to maintain operational continuity.
- **Cost Considerations:** Vessels with dynamic power management can make informed decisions regarding energy sources based on cost factors. This includes choosing energy sources that are economically advantageous at a given moment, contributing to cost-effective operations.
- **Environmental Responsibility:** By intelligently managing power sources, vessels reduce their carbon footprint and minimise emissions. This aligns with sustainability goals and regulatory compliance, supporting the industry's commitment to environmental responsibility.
- **Operational Resilience:** Dynamic power management enhances operational resilience by ensuring vessels can adapt to changing conditions, including weather patterns and fuel availability. This is particularly crucial for vessels navigating unpredictable environments.
- **Resource Optimisation:** These systems optimise resource utilisation by using available energy sources most efficiently. This contributes to resource conservation and sustainability objectives.

Dynamic power management, facilitated by energy storage systems, is a game-changing strategy for enhancing operational flexibility in the maritime industry. It empowers vessels to make informed decisions about energy source selection, optimising efficiency, cost-effectiveness, and environmental responsibility. By seamlessly transitioning between energy sources based on real-time conditions, vessels are better equipped to navigate the challenges of a rapidly changing world while reducing their carbon footprint.

4. SHORE POWER INTEGRATION:

Shore power integration, facilitated by energy storage systems, represents a pivotal strategy for reducing emissions and noise pollution in port areas while enhancing the sustainability of maritime operations.

CLEAN ELECTRICITY FROM PORTS

Shore power (cold ironing or alternative maritime power (AMP)) allows vessels to connect to clean electricity from onshore facilities while berthed at ports. Energy storage systems play a crucial role in enabling and optimising this integration, offering several key advantages:

- **Emissions Reduction:** When vessels connect to shore power, they can switch off their onboard generators, often powered by conventional fossil fuels. This transition to clean, shore-based electricity significantly reduces emissions of greenhouse gases (GHGs), nitrogen oxides (NOx), sulphur oxides (SOx), and particulate matter (PM), contributing to improved air quality and environmental sustainability in port areas.
- **Noise Reduction:** Shore power integration eliminates the noise pollution associated with onboard generators. This benefits port workers and nearby communities by providing a quieter and more pleasant environment.
- **Local Air Quality Improvement:** By reducing emissions within port areas, shore power integration improves local air quality. This is particularly significant in densely populated urban port regions, where air pollution can have adverse health effects.
- **Regulatory Compliance:** Many ports and regulatory bodies require vessels to use shore power to minimise their environmental impact while in port. Energy storage systems facilitate compliance with these regulations, ensuring that vessels can connect to clean electricity efficiently.
- **Operational Efficiency:** Energy storage systems can store excess shore-based electricity when available and discharge it as needed, ensuring a consistent and reliable power supply for vessels at berth. This contributes to operational efficiency and reliability.

Shore power integration, empowered by energy storage systems, is a pivotal strategy for reducing emissions and noise pollution in port areas. It aligns with environmental regulations, enhances air quality, and demonstrates a commitment to eco-conscious practices within the maritime industry. By transitioning to clean electricity while berthed, vessels contribute to a more sustainable and responsible maritime sector.

5. COMPLIANCE WITH EMISSION REGULATIONS:

Compliance with emission regulations is a top priority for the maritime industry, as it seeks to reduce its environmental impact and meet increasingly stringent emission reduction targets. Energy storage solutions are critical in helping vessels achieve compliance and avoid penalties associated with emissions violations.

EMISSION REDUCTION TARGETS

Numerous regions and international organisations have implemented or are in the process of implementing strict regulations to curb greenhouse gas emissions from maritime shipping. These regulations often include caps on emissions of greenhouse gases such as carbon dioxide (CO_2), sulphur oxides (SO_x), nitrogen oxides (NO_x), and particulate matter (PM). Energy storage solutions contribute significantly to achieving compliance with these targets:

- **Emission Mitigation:** Energy storage systems enable vessels to reduce reliance on traditional fossil fuels for propulsion and onboard operations. By utilising renewable energy sources and stored energy, vessels can significantly cut their emissions of GHGs and air pollutants, aligning with emission reduction targets.
- **Efficiency Improvements:** Energy storage solutions enhance the operational efficiency of vessels. They allow for optimising power usage and reducing fuel consumption and emissions during voyages. This not only supports compliance but also contributes to cost savings.
- **Regulatory Alignment:** Energy storage solutions facilitate compliance with emission regulations by allowing vessels to reduce their environmental footprint and align with regional and international emission reduction targets.
- **Penalty Avoidance:** Failure to comply with emission regulations can result in significant penalties for vessel operators. Energy storage systems help vessels avoid such penalties by ensuring compliance with emission limits.
- **Environmental Responsibility:** Compliance with emission regulations reflects a commitment to environmental responsibility. It showcases the maritime industry's dedication to reducing its impact on the environment and mitigating climate change.

Energy storage solutions are instrumental in helping vessels meet emission reduction targets and comply with stringent regulations. They provide the means to reduce emissions, improve operational efficiency, and avoid penalties associated with emissions violations. By integrating these technologies, the maritime industry demonstrates its commitment to responsible and sustainable shipping practices while contributing to global efforts to combat climate change.

6. Economic Savings:

Economic savings are a compelling incentive for maritime companies to adopt energy storage solutions and transition to more sustainable and cost-effective operational practices. One of the most significant avenues for these savings is through fuel cost reduction:

FUEL COST REDUCTION

Ships traditionally rely on conventional fossil fuels, which can represent a substantial portion of their operational expenses. Energy storage systems enable vessels to reduce their dependence on these expensive fuels and tap into renewable energy sources, resulting in several notable economic benefits:

- **Fuel Cost Savings:** By incorporating energy storage systems that harness renewable energy sources, vessels can significantly reduce their fuel consumption. This leads to direct cost savings in fuel procurement, which can be substantial, particularly for long-haul and large vessels.
- **Operational Efficiency:** Energy storage solutions contribute to the overall operational efficiency of vessels. They enable vessels to optimise their energy usage, reducing the need for high-power output from fossil fuel generators and thus minimising fuel consumption.
- **Long-Term Economic Viability:** Reducing fuel costs by adopting energy storage systems enhances the long-term economic viability of maritime operations. It positions companies to navigate fluctuations in fuel prices and market conditions more effectively.
- **Competitive Advantage:** Companies that invest in energy storage solutions and realise fuel cost savings gain a competitive advantage by offering more cost-effective transportation services. This can lead to increased market share and improved profitability.
- **Economic Resilience:** Lower fuel costs improve the financial resilience of maritime companies. They are better prepared to withstand economic challenges and market uncertainties, ensuring continued success.
- **Environmental Responsibility and Brand Image:** Achieving fuel cost reduction through sustainable practices aligns with environmental responsibility, which can enhance a company's brand image and reputation. It attracts environmentally conscious customers and investors.

Energy storage solutions offer substantial economic savings for maritime companies by reducing fuel costs and enhancing operational efficiency. These savings contribute to long-term economic viability, competitive advantage, and financial resilience. They also align with environmental responsibility, making maritime companies more attractive to a wide range of stakeholders, from customers to investors, as they demonstrate a financial and environmental sustainability commitment.

7. EMERGENCY BACKUP POWER:

Emergency backup power is critical to maritime safety, ensuring vessels can respond effectively to engine failures and other emergencies. Energy storage systems play a vital role in providing reliable backup power, enhancing vessel safety, and reducing the risk of incidents at sea.

RELIABILITY:

Enhanced Safety: Emergency backup power supplied by energy storage systems is highly reliable. These systems can rapidly activate and supply power in case of engine failure or other critical emergencies, helping maintain essential vessel functions, such as navigation, communication, and emergency lighting. This enhances crew safety and the safety of the vessel itself.

- **Reduced Risk of Incidents:** Having a dependable backup power source mitigates the risk of incidents at sea that can result from engine failures or power outages. It allows vessels to maintain control and communication, reducing the likelihood of accidents, collisions, or stranding.
- **Environmental Protection:** In situations where engine failure could lead to environmental damage, such as oil spills, backup power ensures that critical pollution prevention and response systems remain operational. This minimises the environmental impact of emergencies.
- **Regulatory Compliance:** Many maritime regulations require vessels to have reliable backup power sources to ensure safety and environmental protection. Energy storage systems help vessels meet these compliance requirements.
- **Operational Continuity:** Energy storage systems support operational continuity during routine maintenance or planned power shutdowns. They can seamlessly provide power to essential systems while main engines are temporarily offline.

Emergency backup power supplied by energy storage systems is crucial to maritime safety. It ensures the reliability of critical systems in emergencies, reduces the risk of incidents, protects the environment, and supports regulatory compliance. By providing a dependable backup power source, energy storage systems enhance the safety and resilience of vessels at sea.

8. SUSTAINABLE REPUTATION:

Building and maintaining a sustainable reputation is valuable for shipping companies in today's environmentally conscious world. Embracing energy storage and renewable energy sources contributes significantly to this reputation, positioning shipping companies as eco-conscious and socially responsible entities. This, in turn, appeals to environmentally conscious customers and investors.

ECO-CONSCIOUS SHIPPING:

- **Environmental Stewardship:** Shipping companies that adopt energy storage and renewable energy solutions demonstrate their commitment to environmental stewardship. This commitment resonates with individuals, organisations, and governments prioritising sustainability and environmental protection.
- **Reduced Carbon Footprint:** Energy storage systems and renewable energy sources reduce a company's carbon footprint and environmental impact. This aligns with global efforts to combat climate change and protect the planet, a shared goal of many stakeholders.
- **Customer Attraction:** Many consumers and businesses prefer to support eco-conscious brands. Shipping companies with a sustainable reputation are more likely to attract environmentally conscious customers who seek to minimise their carbon footprint by choosing greener transportation options.
- **Investor Confidence:** Investors increasingly consider environmental, social, and governance (ESG) factors when making investment decisions. Shipping companies with a strong sustainability track record appeal more to investors who want to align their investments with their values.
- **Competitive Advantage:** A sustainable reputation can provide a competitive advantage in the shipping industry. It differentiates a company from competitors and positions it as a responsible and forward-thinking player in the market.
- **Regulatory Compliance:** Embracing sustainable practices helps shipping companies stay ahead of evolving environmental regulations. It reduces the risk of non-compliance and associated penalties.
- **Community Engagement:** Shipping companies with a sustainable reputation often engage with local communities and environmental organisations to demonstrate their commitment to responsible practices. This fosters positive relationships and goodwill.

A sustainable reputation built on eco-conscious shipping practices, including adopting energy storage and renewable energy sources, has numerous benefits. It attracts environmentally conscious customers and investors, enhances competitiveness, and demonstrates a commitment to environmental stewardship and regulatory compliance. Shipping companies prioritising sustainability are better positioned for long-term success in a world increasingly focused on responsible and environmentally friendly business practices.

9. RESEARCH AND DEVELOPMENT:

Research and development efforts in pursuing energy storage solutions for renewable shipping have far-reaching implications for the maritime sector. These endeavours drive technological advancements, foster innovation, and contribute significantly to sustainability in the industry.

TECHNOLOGICAL ADVANCEMENTS:

- **Clean Propulsion Technologies:** Research and development in energy storage solutions pave the way for cleaner and more sustainable propulsion technologies. This includes developing advanced battery systems, hydrogen fuel cells, and other energy storage technologies tailored for maritime applications.
- **Renewable Integration:** These efforts facilitate the seamless integration of renewable energy sources, such as wind, solar, and hydropower, into maritime operations. Innovative solutions enable vessels to harness the power of these sources efficiently.
- **Energy Efficiency:** Research and development initiatives focus on enhancing the energy efficiency of maritime vessels. This includes optimising power management systems, designing more aerodynamic hulls, and developing energy-efficient propulsion systems.
- **Environmental Sensors:** The maritime industry benefits from research into environmental sensors that monitor air and water quality. These sensors help vessels comply with environmental regulations and minimise their impact on marine ecosystems.
- **Digital Technologies:** Research drives the adoption of digital technologies, such as IoT sensors and data analytics, for vessel optimisation. These technologies enable data-driven decisions that improve energy efficiency, reduce emissions, and enhance safety.
- **Safety Innovations:** Technological advancements in energy storage and renewable shipping enhance safety features and emergency response capabilities on board vessels. This ensures crew and cargo safety, reducing the risk of accidents.
- **Regulatory Compliance:** Developing cleaner propulsion technologies and emission reduction solutions align with evolving environmental regulations. Research and development initiatives help shipping companies meet regulatory requirements effectively.
- **Cost Reduction:** Ongoing research into energy storage solutions leads to cost reductions through improved efficiency, longer lifespan, and economies of scale. This makes sustainable technologies more accessible to a broader range of maritime operators.

Research and development efforts in pursuing energy storage solutions for renewable shipping catalyse innovation and sustainability in the maritime sector. These initiatives drive technological advancements that benefit the environment, enhance operational efficiency, improve safety, and ensure compliance with evolving regulations. They position the maritime industry as a leader in adopting eco-conscious technologies and practices, contributing to a more sustainable and responsible future.

10. LONG-TERM VIABILITY:

The long-term viability of maritime companies is closely tied to their ability to adapt to changing global dynamics, including the transition to cleaner energy sources and stricter environmental regulations. Integrating energy storage into shipping operations represents a strategic move that future-proofs these companies and ensures their competitiveness in an evolving industry landscape.

FUTURE-PROOFING:

- **Environmental Responsibility:** Future-proofing through energy storage aligns with the growing global emphasis on environmental responsibility. Companies that demonstrate their commitment to sustainability are better positioned to meet evolving customer and regulatory expectations.
- **Market Relevance:** As consumers and businesses increasingly prioritise eco-conscious products and services, maritime companies with sustainable practices are more relevant and appealing. This relevance enhances their market position and customer loyalty.
- **Global Trends:** The global trend towards cleaner energy sources and reduced emissions will continue and intensify. Maritime companies integrating energy storage are well-prepared to thrive in this future energy landscape.
- **Operational Efficiency:** Energy storage solutions contribute to operational efficiency and cost savings, enhancing a company's ability to effectively navigate economic challenges and market fluctuations.
- **Regulatory Compliance:** Stringent environmental regulations are on the horizon for the maritime industry. Future-proofing through energy storage helps companies stay ahead of these regulations, minimising the risk of non-compliance and associated penalties.
- **Competitive Advantage:** Companies that adopt sustainable and future-focused practices gain a competitive advantage. They differentiate themselves in the market and attract environmentally conscious customers, partners, and investors.
- **Innovation Leadership:** By embracing innovative technologies like energy storage, maritime companies are leaders in innovation and sustainability. This leadership can drive partnerships, collaborations, and industry recognition.
- **Risk Mitigation:** Future-proofing through sustainability practices helps mitigate risks associated with evolving market dynamics, including shifting consumer preferences, resource scarcity, and climate-related challenges.

Integrating energy storage into shipping operations is a strategic move to ensure maritime companies' long-term viability and competitiveness. It positions them to thrive in a changing industry landscape of cleaner energy sources, stringent environmental regulations, and evolving customer expectations. By embracing sustainability and innovation, these companies secure relevance and resilience in an increasingly eco-conscious world.

Energy storage is not just a technological innovation; it's a fundamental enabler of renewable shipping practices. It provides the maritime industry with the tools to reduce its environmental impact, improve operational efficiency, and meet evolving sustainability standards. As renewable shipping becomes increasingly vital in a world focused on green energy and environmental stewardship, energy storage remains at the forefront of this transformation.

INNOVATIONS IN ENERGY STORAGE SYSTEMS FOR MARITIME SHIPPING

Innovations in energy storage systems are shaping the future of sustainable maritime shipping. These advancements are crucial for improving vessel efficiency, reducing emissions, and enhancing the reliability of renewable energy sources. Here are some notable innovations:

1. HIGH-ENERGY-DENSITY BATTERIES:

High-energy-density batteries, particularly solid-state batteries, are ushering in a new era of energy storage technology for maritime applications. Solid-state batteries represent a significant advancement in the field due to their remarkable attributes, and they promise to revolutionise how vessels harness and store energy.

Solid-state batteries are at the forefront of this innovation. These batteries offer several advantages over traditional lithium-ion batteries, making them particularly well-suited for maritime use. One key advantage is their superior energy density, which means they can store more energy in a smaller, lighter package. This characteristic is especially valuable for vessels with critical space and weight considerations.

Furthermore, solid-state batteries excel in terms of safety and durability. They are less prone to overheating and combustion, addressing concerns associated with traditional batteries. This enhanced safety aspect is paramount in maritime environments where the potential risks of fires or accidents must be minimised.

Another compelling feature of solid-state batteries is their rapid charging capability. These batteries can be charged significantly faster than their lithium-ion counterparts, reducing downtime and allowing vessels to operate more efficiently. This recharge speed aligns with maritime operations' demands that often require quick turnarounds.

As solid-state battery technology advances, these batteries are becoming more compact and accessible for maritime applications. Their high-energy-density, safety, and quick-charging properties make them a promising choice for powering propulsion systems, onboard systems, and emergency backup power on vessels. Solid-state batteries exemplify the potential of cutting-edge energy storage technology to transform the maritime industry, enhancing efficiency, safety, and environmental sustainability.

2. ADVANCED FUEL CELLS:

Advanced fuel cells represent a promising avenue for maritime power generation, offering cleaner and more efficient alternatives to traditional combustion engines. Two prominent types of advanced fuel cells, hydrogen fuel cells and ammonia fuel cells, are emerging as transformative technologies in the maritime sector.

Hydrogen fuel cells garner significant attention as an alternative to conventional ship propulsion systems. These fuel cells generate electricity through a chemical reaction between hydrogen and oxygen, with the only byproduct being water vapour. This inherent cleanliness makes hydrogen fuel cells an attractive option for reducing emissions and promoting sustainability in maritime operations.

One of the standout advantages of hydrogen fuel cells is their potential to provide high energy density and extended operating ranges for vessels. They offer a viable solution for long-haul shipping, where efficient and sustainable power generation is paramount.

Ammonia fuel cells represent another frontier in maritime power generation. Ongoing research and development efforts focus on harnessing ammonia as a hydrogen carrier to produce clean and efficient ship power. Ammonia has the advantage of being a readily transportable and storable energy carrier, making it a promising candidate for marine applications.

These advanced fuel cell technologies align with the maritime industry's growing commitment to reducing emissions and minimising environmental impact. They offer a pathway to cleaner, more efficient, and more sustainable maritime operations. By embracing hydrogen and ammonia fuel cells, vessels can significantly contribute to reducing greenhouse gas emissions and enhancing their environmental performance. As these technologies continue to mature, they are poised to play a pivotal role in shaping the future of maritime propulsion and power generation.

3. ENERGY-DENSE SUPERCAPACITORS:

Energy-dense supercapacitors are emerging as a transformative technology in maritime applications, promising higher energy density and remarkable power output. Supercapacitors offer unique capabilities that make them well-suited for specific ship functions, contributing to improved energy efficiency and performance.

Supercapacitors, with their evolving energy storage capabilities, stand out for their ability to rapidly store and release energy. This characteristic is invaluable in maritime contexts, where quick power bursts are often required. These supercapacitors are well-suited for applications such as regenerative braking systems, which capture and store energy during deceleration and then release it when needed for acceleration. This regenerative capability contributes to fuel savings and efficiency, particularly on vessels with variable propulsion demands.

Moreover, supercapacitors excel in meeting peak power demands on ships. They can discharge energy swiftly, providing the necessary power for critical operations during high-load situations. This ensures that vessels maintain their performance and functionality even under demanding conditions.

As supercapacitor technology continues to evolve, it holds great promise for enhancing energy storage solutions in the maritime sector. By offering higher energy density and rapid energy release capabilities, supercapacitors address specific operational challenges faced by ships. They support energy-efficient regenerative systems and enable vessels to meet peak power demands, contributing to improved performance and sustainability in maritime operations. As the maritime industry continues its quest for cleaner and more efficient energy storage solutions, supercapacitors represent an exciting development with the potential to transform ship energy management.

4. FLYWHEEL ENERGY STORAGE:

Flywheel energy storage is gaining prominence as a robust and efficient technology in maritime applications, with advanced composite flywheels leading the way in achieving high rotational speeds and significant energy storage capacities. These innovative systems provide rapid response times, making them invaluable for addressing power fluctuations in ship operations.

Advanced flywheel energy storage systems leverage composite materials to create flywheels that achieve exceptionally high rotational speeds. This capability allows them to store substantial amounts of energy in a compact and lightweight package, making them well-suited for maritime use where space and weight considerations are critical.

One of the standout features of flywheel energy storage is its rapid response time. These systems can swiftly release stored energy when needed, making them ideal for addressing ship power fluctuations. They provide immediate power during critical moments, ensuring vessels can maintain essential functions and safety measures without interruptions.

Composite flywheels, in particular, offer enhanced performance and durability. Their ability to spin at high speeds and efficiently store energy makes them reliable maritime power management components. They can capture surplus energy during periods of excess power generation and release it during high-demand situations, contributing to improved energy efficiency and ship stability.

As advanced composite flywheels evolve, they hold significant promise for maritime energy storage solutions. Their combination of high rotational speeds, energy storage capacities, and rapid response times addresses operational challenges faced by vessels, supporting a more efficient and reliable energy management system. In an industry increasingly focused on sustainability and performance, flywheel energy storage emerges as a technology poised to enhance the resilience and efficiency of maritime operations.

5. THERMAL ENERGY STORAGE:

Thermal energy storage, particularly utilising phase-change materials (PCMs), offers a versatile and efficient solution for managing thermal energy on ships. PCMs are materials that can store and release thermal energy efficiently through a phase transition, typically changing from a solid to a liquid state or vice versa. In maritime applications, PCMs are increasingly being adopted to store excess heat generated by engines or renewable sources and release it when needed to support onboard systems and enhance energy efficiency.

The key feature of PCMs is their ability to store thermal energy at a constant temperature during a phase transition. When excess heat is available from engine operation or renewable energy sources like solar panels, PCMs absorb this heat and undergo a phase change, transitioning from a solid to a liquid state. This process effectively stores the thermal energy within the PCM.

During times when onboard systems or processes require additional heat, the PCM can release the stored energy by transitioning back from a liquid to a solid state. This controlled release of thermal energy ensures a constant and stable temperature, making it suitable for various applications, including space heating, hot water production, and temperature regulation.

ON SHIPS, THERMAL ENERGY STORAGE USING PCMS OFFERS SEVERAL ADVANTAGES:

- **Energy Efficiency:** PCMs enhance energy efficiency by capturing and reusing excess heat, reducing the overall energy consumption of the vessel.
- **Resource Optimisation:** By storing thermal energy, ships can better manage their power generation resources, optimising engine operation and reducing fuel consumption.
- **Environmental Benefits:** The use of PCMs aligns with sustainability goals by reducing the environmental impact of marine operations through improved energy management.
- **Flexibility:** PCMs are versatile and adaptable to different thermal energy storage needs, making them suitable for a range of maritime applications.

In summary, thermal energy storage with phase-change materials is an innovative approach to efficiently managing thermal energy on ships. By capturing and releasing heat as needed, PCMs improve maritime operations' energy efficiency, resource optimisation, and environmental sustainability. Their flexibility and reliability make them a valuable addition to the evolving landscape of maritime energy storage solutions.

6. LITHIUM-SULPHUR BATTERIES:

Lithium-sulphur batteries significantly advance energy storage technology, particularly in the maritime sector. These batteries are characterised by their unique lithium-sulphur chemistry, which offers several notable advantages over traditional lithium-ion batteries. Their lightweight nature and higher energy density make them a promising choice for maritime applications, where endurance and efficiency are paramount.

The key feature of lithium-sulphur batteries is their chemistry, which replaces the traditional cathode material found in lithium-ion batteries with sulphur. This substitution results in several noteworthy benefits:

- **Lightweight:** Lithium-sulphur batteries are inherently lighter than their lithium-ion counterparts. This weight reduction is a significant advantage in maritime applications, where reducing the vessel's weight can lead to improved fuel efficiency and overall performance.
- **Higher Energy Density:** Lithium-sulphur batteries offer a higher energy density, meaning they can store more energy in a given volume or weight. This attribute translates into longer endurance between charges for maritime vessels, allowing them to operate for extended periods without requiring frequent recharging.

- **Reduced Environmental Impact:** Using sulphur in lithium-sulphur batteries can reduce environmental impact compared to other battery chemistries. This aligns with the maritime industry's increasing focus on sustainability and eco-friendly practices.
- **Longevity:** Lithium-sulphur batteries have the potential for longer cycle life compared to some lithium-ion batteries. This longevity is advantageous for maritime vessels, as it reduces the frequency of battery replacements and associated maintenance costs.

While lithium-sulphur batteries hold great promise for maritime applications, ongoing research and development efforts aim to address challenges such as cycle life and stability. As these challenges are overcome, lithium-sulphur batteries are expected to play a pivotal role in enhancing maritime operations' endurance, efficiency, and sustainability. Their combination of lightweight design and high energy density positions them as a key technology in the evolution of maritime energy storage solutions.

7. BATTERY MANAGEMENT SYSTEMS (BMS):

Battery management systems (BMS) play a crucial role in the efficient and safe operation of energy storage systems, including batteries used in maritime applications. These systems are evolving rapidly, with a notable trend being integrating artificial intelligence (AI) to create AI-powered BMS. These advanced BMS solutions are designed to optimise various aspects of battery performance, leading to extended battery life, enhanced safety, and improved overall efficiency.

The incorporation of AI in BMS represents a significant leap forward in battery technology management, offering several key benefits for maritime applications:

- **Optimised Charging and Discharging:** AI-powered BMS leverages machine learning algorithms to analyse battery performance data continuously. This real-time analysis enables the system to adjust dynamically to charging and discharging patterns. By optimising these processes, AI helps maximise energy storage efficiency, ensuring that batteries are charged and discharged in the most energy-efficient manner possible.
- **Battery Life Extension:** AI-driven BMS can predict and mitigate factors that may lead to battery degradation. By closely monitoring the battery's state of health and considering external factors such as temperature and load profiles, the system can implement strategies to extend the overall lifespan of batteries. This contributes to reduced maintenance and replacement costs for maritime vessels.
- **Enhanced Safety:** Safety is paramount in maritime operations. AI-powered BMS continuously monitors battery conditions and can detect anomalies or potential issues, such as overheating or excessive voltage fluctuations. When such issues are identified, the system can take proactive measures, such as adjusting the charging rate or initiating safety protocols, to prevent critical failures or hazards.
- **Efficient Energy Management:** Energy efficiency is critical for maritime vessels, and AI-powered BMS plays a key role in achieving it. By intelligently managing the energy flow, these systems ensure that energy is utilised optimally to meet propulsion and onboard system needs, reducing waste and improving overall vessel efficiency.

- **Data-Driven Insights:** AI-powered BMS generates valuable data and insights about battery performance over time. This data can inform decisions about maintenance schedules, replacement strategies, and future energy storage system upgrades, enabling more informed and cost-effective management of maritime energy systems.

AI-powered BMS represents a significant advancement in energy storage technology for maritime applications. By harnessing the capabilities of artificial intelligence, these systems optimise charging and discharging, extend battery life, enhance safety, improve energy efficiency, and provide valuable data-driven insights. As the maritime industry continues to embrace innovative energy storage solutions, AI-powered BMS stands out as a crucial component in ensuring the reliability and sustainability of onboard energy systems.

8. MODULAR AND SCALABLE SOLUTIONS:

Modular and scalable energy storage solutions are transforming the maritime industry, offering vessels greater flexibility and adaptability in managing energy needs. One notable feature of these solutions is swappable battery modules, which enable vessels to easily replace and scale their energy storage capacity to align with specific operational requirements.

Modular energy storage involves dividing a vessel's energy storage system into interchangeable units or modules. Each module contains a set of batteries and associated components. These modules can be easily swapped in and out of the energy storage system as needed, allowing for efficient maintenance and upgrades without significant downtime.

One significant advantage of modular systems is their adaptability to maritime operators. Vessels can adjust their energy storage capacity based on changing operational demands. For example, vessels can quickly add or replace modules to boost their available energy during periods of higher power demand, such as when navigating through challenging conditions or requiring bursts of additional propulsion. Conversely, during reduced demand, they can remove modules to reduce weight and optimise efficiency.

Swappable battery modules contribute to improved vessel performance and operational resilience. In cases of battery degradation or failure, replacing a single module is far more efficient and cost-effective than replacing an entire energy storage system. This minimises downtime and maintenance costs while ensuring the vessel remains operational.

Furthermore, modular and scalable solutions align with the broader trend toward sustainable and eco-friendly maritime practices. Vessels can optimise their energy storage capacity to reduce emissions, enhance fuel efficiency, and minimise environmental impact during their voyages.

Modular and scalable energy storage solutions, including swappable battery modules, provide maritime vessels with the adaptability needed to meet specific operational requirements. These systems offer efficiency, flexibility, and cost-effectiveness, improving vessel performance and sustainability. As the maritime industry continues to embrace innovative energy storage technologies, modular and scalable solutions stand out as a key enabler of efficient and resilient energy management on board ships.

9. ADVANCED THERMAL MANAGEMENT:

Advanced thermal management systems are pivotal in optimising energy storage solutions' performance and safety, particularly in the maritime industry. These systems are designed to maintain optimal temperature conditions for batteries and other components, ensuring they operate efficiently and reliably in the often-challenging maritime environment.

One of the primary goals of advanced thermal management is to enhance thermal efficiency. Batteries perform best within a specific temperature range, and maintaining this range is critical to their overall performance and lifespan. Innovative thermal management systems achieve this by actively regulating the temperature of the battery cells. They can dissipate excess heat generated during charging and discharging, preventing overheating and thermal runaway. Conversely, they can provide heating when necessary to ensure batteries operate optimally in cold conditions.

In maritime applications, where vessels may encounter extreme temperatures and variable environmental conditions, advanced thermal management is essential. It ensures that energy storage systems consistently deliver the required power and energy, regardless of external factors. Moreover, by maintaining batteries within their ideal temperature range, these systems contribute to the longevity and durability of the energy storage system, reducing the need for frequent replacements and maintenance.

Safety is another critical aspect of advanced thermal management. By preventing excessive temperature fluctuations and managing heat effectively, these systems reduce the risk of thermal events or battery-related accidents. This is especially crucial in maritime operations, where safety and reliability are paramount.

Advanced thermal management systems are a cornerstone of modern energy storage technology in the maritime industry. They enhance the efficiency and safety of batteries by maintaining optimal temperature conditions, ensuring reliable performance even in challenging maritime environments. As vessels increasingly rely on energy storage solutions for their power needs, these innovative thermal management systems enable efficient and safe energy storage operations on board ships.

10. AUTONOMOUS ENERGY MANAGEMENT:

Autonomous energy management is ushering in a new era of efficiency and sustainability in maritime operations, and at its core is the integration of AI-based energy management systems. These sophisticated algorithms are designed to revolutionise how vessels store, manage, and utilise energy by leveraging real-time data, weather conditions, and operational requirements to ensure the most efficient use of available energy resources.

AI-based energy management represents a paradigm shift in maritime energy storage and utilisation. These systems continuously analyse many factors, including the vessel's current energy reserves, power demand, weather forecasts, and route information. By processing this data in real time, they make dynamic decisions regarding energy storage, distribution, and consumption.

One of the primary advantages of autonomous energy management is its ability to optimise energy utilisation. AI algorithms can balance the power requirements of propulsion systems, onboard systems, and auxiliary equipment, ensuring that energy is allocated where it's needed most. This enhances overall vessel efficiency and reduces fuel consumption and emissions by minimising energy waste.

Moreover, these systems are designed to adapt to changing conditions. For instance, if a vessel encounters adverse weather conditions that require increased propulsion power, the AI-based energy management system can adjust energy distribution accordingly. Conversely, during periods of lower power demand, the system can store excess energy for future use, contributing to energy savings.

The safety and reliability of autonomous energy management systems are also noteworthy. They can continuously monitor the health of the energy storage system, detecting potential issues or anomalies and taking proactive measures to mitigate risks. This proactive approach enhances vessel safety and reduces the likelihood of power-related failures or disruptions during critical operations.

In the maritime industry, where the demand for greater efficiency and sustainability is growing, autonomous energy management powered by AI offers a transformative solution. These systems enable vessels to operate precisely, minimising energy waste, reducing fuel consumption, and adhering to environmental regulations. As the maritime sector continues to embrace innovative energy management practices, AI-based energy management systems stand out as a game-changer, driving efficiency, sustainability, and operational excellence in maritime operations.

11. MULTI-MODAL ENERGY SOURCES:

Multi-modal energy sources are ushering in a new era of flexibility, redundancy, and enhanced reliability in maritime energy supply. One of the key approaches in this domain is the development of hybrid energy systems, which seamlessly combine multiple energy sources, including batteries, fuel cells, and renewable generators. These systems offer a multifaceted solution to meet the diverse energy needs of vessels, ultimately increasing operational reliability and efficiency.

Hybrid energy systems are designed to leverage the strengths of each energy source while mitigating their weaknesses. Batteries, for instance, excel in providing quick bursts of power and can capture surplus energy for later use. Fuel cells offer a stable and continuous power source with minimal emissions, making them well-suited for longer voyages. Renewable generators, such as solar panels and wind turbines, harness clean energy from nature, contributing to sustainability.

Fusing these energy sources creates a versatile energy ecosystem on board vessels. During periods of high power demand, the system can draw from batteries for instant power delivery. In scenarios where a stable, long-term power supply is required, fuel cells can take over, ensuring uninterrupted operations. Renewable generators complement these sources by harnessing energy from the environment, reducing reliance on conventional fuels.

One of the standout advantages of multi-modal energy sources is redundancy. Vessels equipped with hybrid systems have built-in backup options. If one energy source encounters an issue, the system can seamlessly switch to another, ensuring continuous power supply. This redundancy enhances vessel reliability, a critical factor in maritime operations.

Furthermore, the efficiency gains of hybrid systems are notable. By optimising the use of different energy sources based on the vessel's operational needs, these systems reduce energy waste and fuel consumption. This, in turn, contributes to cost savings and environmental sustainability.

In an era where the maritime industry is embracing eco-friendly practices and striving for greater operational efficiency, multi-modal energy sources and hybrid energy systems emerge as a game-changing solutions. They offer versatility, reliability, and efficiency, enabling vessels to navigate diverse operational challenges while reducing their environmental footprint. As vessels continue to explore innovative energy supply options, multi-modal energy sources represent a pivotal development in maritime energy management.

12. GREEN HYDROGEN STORAGE:

Green hydrogen storage, particularly through Liquid Organic Hydrogen Carriers (LOHCs), presents a promising avenue for the maritime industry to transition towards cleaner and more sustainable fuel sources. LOHCs offer a safe, efficient, and versatile method for storing and transporting green hydrogen, which can be used as a clean and eco-friendly fuel source in maritime applications.

At its core, green hydrogen is produced through water electrolysis using renewable energy sources such as wind or solar power. This production process yields hydrogen entirely free from carbon emissions, positioning it as a clean alternative to traditional fossil fuels.

However, one of the key challenges with hydrogen is its storage and transportation. This is where Liquid Organic Hydrogen Carriers (LOHCs) come into play. LOHCs are chemical compounds that bond with hydrogen molecules, effectively "capturing" and storing them in a liquid solution. This solution can then be transported and stored at ambient temperatures and pressures, simplifying the logistics of hydrogen transport compared to high-pressure gas storage.

THE USE OF LOHCS OFFERS SEVERAL ADVANTAGES FOR MARITIME APPLICATIONS:

- **Efficient Hydrogen Storage:** LOHCs enable dense hydrogen storage, making it a practical solution for vessels with limited space and weight constraints. This allows ships to carry substantial green hydrogen for extended voyages.
- **Safety:** LOHCs provide a safer means of hydrogen storage than high-pressure gas storage, as they are not prone to leakage or explosions. This enhances safety on board maritime vessels.
- **Versatility:** Green hydrogen stored in LOHCs can be easily converted back into gaseous hydrogen when needed, making it suitable for a wide range of maritime propulsion systems, including fuel cells and combustion engines.
- **Environmental Benefits:** The use of green hydrogen produced from renewable sources aligns with the maritime industry's sustainability goals, reducing greenhouse gas emissions and contributing to cleaner maritime operations.

As the maritime sector continues exploring sustainable and low-emission alternatives, green hydrogen storage with LOHCs is a promising solution. It addresses the challenges of hydrogen storage and transport while offering vessels a clean and efficient energy source. The adoption of this technology has the potential to drive the maritime industry closer to its sustainability objectives while ensuring reliable and environmentally friendly energy storage and utilisation on board ships.

These innovations are transforming energy storage systems for maritime shipping, making vessels more sustainable, efficient, and environmentally friendly. As the maritime industry continues its transition toward renewable energy sources, these technologies will play a crucial role in shaping the future of sustainable shipping.

EFFECTIVE ENERGY MANAGEMENT STRATEGIES IN MARITIME SHIPPING

Effective energy management is paramount in maritime shipping for reducing fuel consumption, emissions, and operational costs while ensuring reliable and sustainable operations. In the shipping industry, several key strategies have emerged as critical components of efficient energy management:

1. **Integrated Energy Management Systems:** Implementing comprehensive energy management systems that monitor and control all aspects of energy consumption onboard vessels, including propulsion, lighting, HVAC, and auxiliary systems, is crucial. Real-time data from sensors and monitoring systems provide insights into energy performance, enabling informed decision-making.
2. **Voyage Planning and Route Optimisation:** Optimal routing takes into account weather conditions, currents, and the most fuel-efficient paths. Digital navigation tools continuously optimise routes during transit, while speed management adjusts vessel speed based on route, weather, and fuel efficiency considerations.

3. **Load Management:** Load management involves peak shaving to balance energy loads, preventing peak power demands and reducing generator strain and fuel consumption. Additionally, cargo handling procedures can be optimised to minimise energy-intensive operations.
4. **Fuel-Efficient Propulsion:** Utilising variable pitch propellers to optimise propulsion efficiency based on vessel speed and load conditions, and maintaining optimal vessel trim, reduces hydrodynamic resistance and enhances fuel efficiency.
5. **Energy Storage Integration:** Integrating energy storage systems, such as batteries or flywheels, allows vessels to store excess energy from renewable sources and provide backup power during peak demand. Hybrid propulsion systems combining traditional engines with energy storage offer higher efficiency and lower emissions.
6. **Alternative Fuels and Clean Technologies:** Considering LNG conversion or other low-emission fuels helps reduce greenhouse gas emissions. Incorporating wind-assisted propulsion systems and solar panels harnesses renewable energy sources, reducing reliance on conventional fuels.
7. **Regular Maintenance and Efficiency Audits:** Scheduled maintenance ensures shipboard systems operate efficiently, reducing energy waste. Efficiency audits identify areas for improvement and guide corrective measures.
8. **Crew Training and Awareness:** Training programs educate crew members on energy-efficient practices and emphasise the importance of reducing energy consumption and emissions. Fostering an energy-conscious culture encourages crew members to identify and report energy-saving opportunities.
9. **Regulatory Compliance and Emission Reduction:** Meeting international and national emissions regulations often involves installing emission reduction technologies like exhaust gas cleaning systems (scrubbers). Compliance with the Energy Efficiency Existing Ship Index (EEXI) requires implementing energy-efficient measures on existing vessels to reduce carbon intensity.
10. **Continuous Improvement and Innovation:** Data-driven decision-making involves collecting and analysing data to identify trends, assess the impact of energy-saving measures, and explore new efficiency opportunities. Investment in research and development fosters innovation and the exploration of technologies that improve vessel energy efficiency.

By implementing these energy management strategies, maritime shipping companies can reduce their environmental impact, enhance operational efficiency, and navigate the path toward a more sustainable and cost-effective future in the industry. These strategies are integral to addressing the evolving challenges and opportunities in maritime energy management.

Chapter 13

ENVIRONMENTAL IMPACT ASSESSMENT

Environmental Impact Assessment (EIA) is a critical and systematic process integral to the maritime shipping industry. Its primary purpose is to rigorously evaluate and analyse the potential environmental repercussions stemming from various shipping activities and the development and expansion of maritime infrastructure. Within this chapter, we delve into the profound significance of EIAs within the maritime domain, shedding light on their multifaceted components, meticulous methodologies, and the pivotal role they assume in steering the industry towards a future characterised by sustainability, environmental stewardship, and responsible operational practices.

As maritime activities expand and evolve, the need for comprehensive EIAs has become increasingly evident. These assessments serve as a crucial pillar of maritime governance, aiding in identifying, understanding, and mitigating environmental challenges associated with shipping operations and the associated infrastructure. Through systematic evaluation, EIAs ensure that shipping entities and infrastructure projects uphold their environmental responsibilities, fostering a harmonious coexistence with the marine ecosystem and surrounding communities. In this chapter, we embark on a journey to explore the depth of EIAs within maritime shipping, unravelling their various facets and unveiling their instrumental role in steering the industry towards a sustainable and responsible future.

METHODS FOR EVALUATING THE ENVIRONMENTAL IMPACT OF SHIPPING OPERATIONS

Evaluating the environmental impact of shipping operations requires a comprehensive and systematic approach. Several methods and techniques are employed to assess various aspects of these impacts, ensuring that maritime activities align with sustainability goals. Here are some of the key methods used:

1. ENVIRONMENTAL IMPACT ASSESSMENT (EIA)

Environmental Impact Assessment (EIA) is a pivotal and multifaceted process that comprehensively examines the potential environmental consequences stemming from distinct shipping projects or activities. This meticulous evaluation extends its purview to encompass a broad spectrum of influential factors, ranging from scrutinising emissions and preserving water quality to safeguarding the delicate equilibrium of marine ecosystems and assessing the socio-economic implications on surrounding communities.

Moreover, it is imperative to underscore that the importance of EIAs transcends national boundaries. Recognising their vital role in upholding environmental responsibility, many countries, in conjunction with international organisations, have enforced stringent regulations mandating the incorporation of EIAs for noteworthy maritime ventures. By ensuring adherence to these environmental standards, EIAs function as a linchpin in navigating the labyrinth of maritime activities, ensuring that sustainability and ecological integrity remain at the forefront of the industry's endeavours. Through the lens of an EIA, the maritime sector endeavours to strike a harmonious balance between fostering economic growth and nurturing the environment upon which it relies.

1. LIFE CYCLE ASSESSMENT (LCA)

Life Cycle Assessment (LCA) emerges as a comprehensive framework, offering an all-encompassing perspective on the environmental ramifications of shipping operations throughout their intricate lifecycle. This meticulous examination spans from the initial phases of ship design and construction, traversing the operational lifespan of vessels, and extending to their eventual decommissioning and environmentally responsible disposal.

Within the realm of LCA, a multifaceted array of critical factors are scrutinised. This encompassing analysis takes into account resource consumption, encompassing the procurement of materials and their utilisation, and meticulously tracks energy consumption patterns. Furthermore, LCA delves into the intricate intricacies of emissions, scrutinising the release of greenhouse gases, sulphur oxides (SOx), nitrogen oxides (NOx), and particulate matter (PM) at each stage of the vessel's existence. Additionally, this comprehensive methodology meticulously evaluates waste generation, assessing the ecological footprint arising from ship-related waste products.

By employing this rigorous analytical framework, LCA facilitates a comprehensive comprehension of the intricate interplay between shipping operations and their environmental consequences. It serves as a fundamental compass guiding the maritime industry towards sustainable practices that minimise resource exploitation, energy inefficiency, and environmental impact across the entire lifecycle of vessels. Through the discerning lens of LCA, the maritime sector endeavours to embrace environmentally responsible practices and steer towards a future marked by ecological equilibrium and resource conservation.

1. ENVIRONMENTAL PERFORMANCE INDICATORS

Environmental Performance Indicators, often called EPIs, constitute a sophisticated and data-driven approach to assess and quantify a vessel's environmental performance. Their primary focus centres around gauging crucial facets, particularly those intertwined with energy efficiency and emissions management, within the intricate realm of maritime operations.

In this realm, these metrics serve as vital barometers of a ship's ecological footprint, affording precise measurements of its energy consumption and emissions output. Prominent examples of these metrics encompass the Energy Efficiency Existing Ship Index (EEXI) and the Energy Efficiency Operational Indicator (EEOI). These refined tools not only offer a lens through which to evaluate the environmental prowess of a vessel but also facilitate a means of comparative analysis.

Companies operating within the maritime sector leverage these indicators as essential yardsticks to benchmark their fleet's performance against industry-established standards. This benchmarking process lays the foundation for a journey towards operational enhancements, underpinned by data-backed insights and eco-conscious strategies. Through the discerning deployment of Environmental Performance Indicators, the maritime industry fosters a culture of continual improvement, orchestrating a harmonious symphony between operational efficiency and environmental stewardship.

1. AIR EMISSION MONITORING

Air emission monitoring is a pivotal discipline encompassing a spectrum of advanced methodologies, all geared towards the meticulous scrutiny of exhaust emissions originating from maritime vessels. These emissions span a diverse range, notably including sulphur oxides (SOx), nitrogen oxides (NOx), and particulate matter (PM), each carrying its distinct ecological ramifications.

Within this realm, the heart of air emission monitoring lies in deploying state-of-the-art sensors and data acquisition systems. These sophisticated instruments are strategically positioned to capture real-time data from the vessel's exhaust systems. This dynamic influx of data is a powerful resource, illuminating the intricacies of emissions patterns, their temporal fluctuations, and the performance of emission abatement technologies.

The significance of air emission monitoring extends beyond mere data collection. It forms the backbone of a proactive approach to emissions reduction within the maritime industry. With insights from real-time data, shipping companies are empowered to fine-tune engine performance, optimise fuel consumption, and curtail emissions. This ongoing process, underpinned by continual monitoring, represents a conscientious stride towards the overarching goal of minimising the environmental footprint of maritime operations while concurrently bolstering operational efficiency. In essence, air emission monitoring weaves together the threads of data, technology, and environmental stewardship, propelling the maritime sector towards a sustainable and eco-conscious future.

1. WATER QUALITY ASSESSMENT

Water quality assessment, as a multidimensional endeavour, encompasses an array of critical facets within the intricate tapestry of marine environmental impact. This multifaceted approach traverses a spectrum of pivotal considerations, offering a meticulous evaluation of the health and integrity of marine ecosystems.

Central to this assessment is monitoring ballast water treatment systems, a pivotal measure to prevent the inadvertent spread of invasive species across various aquatic ecosystems. This vigilance is a vital safeguard, preventing the introduction of non-native species that could disrupt local biodiversity.

Furthermore, water quality assessment delves into routine pollutant monitoring, covering aspects such as detecting oil discharges and sewage effluents. These ongoing assessments, often employing cutting-edge technology and precise testing methodologies, serve as sentinel guardians of marine water quality.

If discrepancies or pollutants are detected, water quality assessments guide the implementation of judicious corrective actions. These measures, born from the insights gleaned through rigorous assessment, are instrumental in preserving and rejuvenating water quality. Through the conscientious practice of water quality assessment, the maritime sector aligns itself with sustainable and ecologically responsible principles, reaffirming its commitment to safeguarding marine ecosystems and ensuring the vitality of aquatic environments for generations to come.

1. NOISE POLLUTION STUDIES

The domain of noise pollution studies is a multifaceted and diligent endeavour centred on assessing and mitigating underwater noise emissions stemming from maritime vessels. The ramifications of such emissions are profound, as they have the potential to disrupt the delicate equilibrium of marine ecosystems and exert adverse effects on the well-being of marine life.

At the core of these studies is the meticulous measurement and analysis of underwater noise levels. Cutting-edge acoustic sensors and data collection systems are strategically deployed to capture and scrutinise the intricate nuances of noise emissions. These data-driven insights provide a profound understanding of the acoustic landscape within marine environments.

Moreover, the findings derived from noise pollution studies serve as catalysts for proactive measures. These measures may encompass deploying innovative noise reduction technologies aboard vessels or strategic adjustments to maritime routes to minimise the ecological impact on marine organisms.

Ultimately, noise pollution studies exemplify a conscientious commitment to ecological stewardship within the maritime sector. By diligently assessing and mitigating the impacts of underwater noise emissions, the industry embarks toward harmonious coexistence with marine life and ecosystems, ensuring their vitality and sustainability in the face of evolving maritime activities.

1. ECOLOGICAL SURVEYS

The realm of ecological surveys emerges as a comprehensive and far-reaching endeavour, meticulously designed to fathom the intricate interplay between shipping activities and the marine ecosystems that serve as their host. This multidimensional assessment casts a discerning eye on the multifaceted aspects of environmental impact within the maritime domain.

At the heart of ecological surveys lies the vigilant monitoring of biodiversity, a fundamental aspect that underscores the health and vitality of marine environments. These surveys encompass a sweeping spectrum, from meticulously cataloguing species diversity to preserving vulnerable habitats that house fragile ecosystems.

Moreover, ecological surveys serve as the harbinger of environmental conservation, wielding the power to detect damage or disruption within marine ecosystems. When such impacts are discerned, these surveys pivot towards proactive measures. This might entail implementing judicious mitigation strategies, such as habitat restoration efforts, designed to rejuvenate and safeguard the ecological sanctity of impacted regions.

In essence, ecological surveys epitomise the maritime industry's commitment to responsible stewardship. Through these meticulous examinations, the industry embarks on a path to harmonise the coexistence of maritime activities and marine ecosystems, fortifying the fragile balance between progress and preservation for the benefit of present and future generations.

1. SOCIAL IMPACT ASSESSMENT

The domain of social impact assessment serves as a bridge connecting maritime endeavours with the communities that are intricately intertwined with them. This multifaceted undertaking involves a dynamic engagement process with local communities to comprehend their perspectives and concerns in maritime operations.

At its core, social impact assessment strives to unravel the intricate tapestry of how maritime activities influence the well-being and fabric of these communities. It meticulously examines the multifaceted dimensions of this impact, which can encompass social, economic, and cultural aspects. By shedding light on these dynamics, it lays the groundwork for informed decision-making and conscientious corporate citizenship.

In doing so, social impact assessment has the potential to identify potential negative repercussions stemming from maritime activities. Armed with this knowledge, it paves the way for the development and implementation of judicious mitigation measures. Furthermore, it explores the concept of benefits sharing, ensuring that communities derive equitable advantages from maritime endeavours.

In essence, social impact assessment represents a profound commitment to harmonising maritime progress with community interests. It seeks to foster an environment where the maritime sector operates not as an external force but as an engaged and responsible neighbour, ensuring that maritime activities' benefits and burdens are equally distributed and that the communities remain integral partners in the journey towards a sustainable future.

1. REMOTE SENSING AND SATELLITE MONITORING

Within the realm of remote sensing and satellite technology lies a formidable arsenal of tools that empower the maritime industry to embrace a proactive approach towards environmental monitoring and regulatory compliance. These cutting-edge methodologies usher in a new era of real-time information and data-driven decision-making.

Central to this paradigm is the real-time tracking of vessel movements, a pivotal facet that affords precise insights into maritime activities. Satellite technology, with its keen eye from above, captures the nuances of ship routes, ensuring compliance with regulations and highlighting deviations when they occur.

Furthermore, this technology extends its reach to the surveillance of emissions, particularly those stemming from exhaust stacks. It offers an unobtrusive vantage point from which to assess the release of pollutants like sulphur oxides (SOx), nitrogen oxides (NOx), and particulate matter (PM) into the atmosphere. This real-time monitoring promotes environmental stewardship and helps navigate the intricate waters of emissions regulations.

Additionally, remote sensing and satellite monitoring provide a robust foundation for proactive environmental monitoring. Through data analytics, deviations and irregularities from environmental regulations are promptly identified, offering an opportunity for rapid corrective action. This capability is instrumental in ensuring that maritime activities align with ecological responsibilities.

In essence, remote sensing and satellite monitoring represent the maritime industry's commitment to harnessing technology for the greater good. They forge a path toward informed, data-driven decision-making, fostering an environment where regulatory compliance and ecological stewardship are paramount. In doing so, they propel the industry towards a future marked by sustainability and harmonious coexistence with the marine environment.

1. SIMULATION AND MODELLING

At the nexus of advanced computational capabilities lies the formidable realm of simulation and modelling, wielding profound influence in the maritime industry's quest for environmental responsibility and operational efficiency. These sophisticated tools offer a dynamic platform for forecasting and mitigating the environmental impact of a spectrum of scenarios, ranging from accidental spills to routine emissions.

Central to this domain are the intricate models that simulate the dispersion of pollutants, offering a virtual laboratory for assessing their behaviour and impact within diverse marine environments. These computational marvels serve as proactive sentinels, enabling the industry to predict and plan for potential environmental challenges, ultimately aiding in formulating robust mitigation strategies.

Beyond crisis response, simulation and modelling extend their utility to route optimisation and operational planning. Through the lens of these digital tools, maritime companies chart pathways that minimise fuel consumption and emissions. By leveraging the power of predictive analytics, they fine-tune voyage plans and vessel operations to strike a harmonious balance between operational efficiency and ecological responsibility.

Simulation and modelling stand as beacons of foresight within the maritime sector. They not only guide the industry in navigating the complex waters of environmental impact but also empower it to optimise operations in alignment with sustainability goals. Through their strategic deployment, the maritime industry embarks on a trajectory characterised by informed decision-making and a steadfast commitment to preserving the marine environment.

These methods mentioned above collectively form a robust toolkit for assessing and mitigating the environmental impact of shipping operations, ensuring sustainable and responsible maritime practices while safeguarding marine ecosystems and communities.

MITIGATION STRATEGIES AND BEST PRACTICES

In pursuing sustainable and environmentally responsible maritime practices, implementing effective mitigation strategies and adherence to best practices are paramount. These strategies encompass a multifaceted approach aimed at reducing the environmental impact of shipping operations while fostering operational efficiency and ecological stewardship.

One fundamental mitigation strategy revolves around adopting cleaner and more fuel-efficient technologies. This includes the utilisation of eco-friendly fuels, such as liquefied natural gas (LNG) and hydrogen, which reduce greenhouse gas emissions and air pollutants. The retrofitting of vessels with advanced emission control systems, such as exhaust gas cleaning systems (scrubbers), also plays a pivotal role in curbing emissions of sulphur oxides (SOx) and nitrogen oxides (NOx).

Furthermore, proactive vessel maintenance and hull cleaning practices are integral to mitigation. Regular hull cleaning reduces hydrodynamic resistance, enhancing fuel efficiency and subsequently reducing emissions. Effective ballast water management systems are deployed to prevent the inadvertent spread of invasive species, safeguarding local ecosystems.

Route optimisation and voyage planning are linchpins in mitigating emissions and fuel consumption. Utilising sophisticated weather routing systems and voyage optimisation software, shipping companies can chart courses that capitalise on favourable weather conditions and ocean currents, minimising fuel use and emissions en route.

Additionally, proactive engagement with local communities and stakeholders is instrumental in addressing social and environmental concerns. Transparency and dialogue help identify potential impacts and allow for developing collaborative mitigation strategies, promoting a harmonious relationship between maritime operations and coastal communities.

In the realm of regulations and compliance, stringent adherence to international and national environmental standards is non-negotiable. Companies are encouraged to stay abreast of evolving regulations and invest in crew training to ensure full compliance.

Mitigation strategies and best practices within the maritime industry are pivotal to achieving sustainable and eco-conscious operations. By embracing cleaner technologies, optimising routes, engaging with communities, and adhering to regulations, the sector can navigate a future where environmental responsibility and operational excellence coexist harmoniously. These practices mitigate environmental impact and position the industry for long-term resilience and success in a changing world.

REGULATORY REQUIREMENTS FOR ENVIRONMENTAL IMPACT ASSESSMENTS

Environmental Impact Assessments (EIAs) in the maritime sector are subject to a web of stringent regulatory requirements at both national and international levels. These regulations are designed to ensure that shipping activities and associated infrastructure developments are conducted with meticulous consideration of their environmental consequences.

On an international scale, the International Maritime Organisation (IMO) has established guidelines and conventions to govern EIAs. The MARPOL Annex VI, for instance, outlines stringent emissions limits for vessels, including sulphur oxide (SOx) and nitrogen oxide (NOx) emissions, which necessitate thorough compliance assessments. The Ballast Water Management Convention sets forth regulations to prevent the spread of invasive species through ballast water discharge, requiring comprehensive assessments of ballast water treatment systems.

Nationally, countries enact their environmental regulations and may mandate EIAs for significant maritime projects. These regulations vary widely but often mirror international standards. For example, the United States has the National Environmental Policy Act (NEPA), which requires federal agencies to assess the environmental impacts of proposed actions, including maritime projects. Similarly, the European Union's Environmental Impact Assessment Directive mandates the assessment of the environmental effects of certain projects, including those related to the maritime sector.

In addition to these broad regulations, specific regions and jurisdictions may impose additional requirements depending on local environmental sensitivities. Coastal states and regions may enforce more stringent regulations to protect their unique marine ecosystems and coastal communities.

Overall, the regulatory landscape for EIAs in maritime shipping is complex and evolving. Compliance with these regulations is essential to meet legal obligations and uphold environmental responsibility and sustainability within the industry. By adhering to these requirements, the maritime sector is committed to minimising its environmental footprint and safeguarding marine ecosystems.

Chapter **14**

MARITIME EDUCATION AND WORKFORCE DEVELOPMENT

The maritime industry is amid a profound transformation driven by the imperative for sustainability and the adoption of green practices. As vessels become more environmentally friendly and regulations evolve, there is an increasing demand for a skilled and knowledgeable workforce to navigate this new era of maritime shipping. Chapter 14 delves into the critical realm of maritime education and workforce development, shedding light on their pivotal role in shaping the industry's future.

This chapter begins by exploring the changing landscape of maritime education. It underscores the need for curricula that reflect the evolving industry, emphasising sustainability, clean technologies, and environmental regulations. It delves into the importance of fostering a new generation of maritime professionals who possess technical expertise and a deep understanding of ecological responsibility.

Moreover, the chapter delves into the pivotal role of vocational training and apprenticeships in nurturing maritime talent. It highlights successful programs and initiatives that bridge the gap between theoretical knowledge and practical skills, producing a workforce ready to embrace the challenges and opportunities presented by green shipping.

Workforce diversity and inclusion are integral aspects discussed within this chapter. It examines efforts to attract a diverse talent pool, ensuring maritime careers are accessible and appealing to individuals of all backgrounds. By embracing diversity, the industry enriches its talent pool and benefits from various perspectives and innovations.

Additionally, this chapter delves into ongoing professional development opportunities for existing maritime professionals. It emphasises the importance of continuous learning and adaptation in an industry characterised by rapid technological advancements and changing regulations.

Lastly, the chapter explores partnerships between educational institutions, maritime companies, and government bodies. Collaborative initiatives are highlighted, demonstrating how joint efforts can yield a workforce that is well-prepared for sustainable shipping challenges and aligned with the industry's commitment to responsible practices.

THE NEED FOR SKILLED PROFESSIONALS IN GREEN SHIPPING

In the evolving landscape of maritime shipping, the need for skilled professionals in green shipping has become more pressing than ever. This demand arises from a confluence of factors, including the imperative for sustainability, adopting renewable energy sources, and tightening environmental regulations. Skilled individuals are essential to navigate this transformation and ensure the industry's responsible and eco-conscious progression.

The transition towards green shipping practices is rapidly reshaping the maritime industry, and with it comes an increasingly urgent need for skilled professionals who can navigate this new era effectively. The need for such professionals stems from the complex and multifaceted nature of sustainable shipping. Green shipping encompasses a wide array of technologies, regulations, and best practices, all aimed at reducing the environmental impact of maritime operations. Skilled individuals are required to not only comprehend these complexities but also to implement them effectively.

One key aspect of this need is a deep understanding of environmental regulations. As international and national regulations governing emissions, ballast water management, and other environmental aspects become more stringent, shipping companies must rely on professionals who can ensure compliance. Skilled individuals are essential for interpreting these regulations, managing the necessary paperwork, and implementing measures to adhere to emission limits and other environmental standards.

Furthermore, adopting green technologies in shipping, such as using alternative fuels, implementing emission reduction technologies, and retrofitting vessels for sustainability, requires professionals who can oversee these transformations. From engineers well-versed in the intricacies of eco-friendly propulsion systems to specialists in retrofitting existing vessels, the industry needs individuals who can drive these technological advancements.

Environmental stewardship is another critical aspect. Professionals understanding the delicate balance between maritime operations and the marine environment are indispensable. They can develop and implement strategies to minimise the impact of shipping activities on local ecosystems, helping to protect marine life and biodiversity.

Moreover, the need for skilled professionals in green shipping extends to the development and execution of sustainability strategies. Companies increasingly recognise that sustainability is a regulatory requirement and a competitive advantage. Professionals who can design and execute sustainability plans, conduct environmental impact assessments, and drive corporate responsibility initiatives are essential to achieving long-term success in the evolving maritime landscape.

The maritime industry's shift towards green shipping practices necessitates a workforce of skilled professionals who can navigate the complexities of sustainability, regulations, technology, and environmental stewardship. These individuals are vital for ensuring compliance, driving innovation and ushering in a more environmentally responsible and sustainable future for the industry.

TRAINING AND EDUCATION PROGRAMS FOR MARITIME PERSONNEL

Training and education programs for maritime personnel are fundamental components of preparing the industry's workforce for the challenges and opportunities of green shipping. These programs equip individuals with the knowledge, skills, and competencies required to excel in a maritime landscape increasingly emphasising sustainability and environmental responsibility.

One of the primary elements of such programs is the inclusion of comprehensive courses on environmental regulations and compliance. These courses cover many topics, including emissions control, ballast water management, and waste disposal regulations. Personnel are trained to understand these regulations' intricacies, ensuring they can navigate the complex web of environmental compliance effectively.

Furthermore, training programs often delve into the realm of green technologies and eco-friendly practices. This includes instruction on the utilisation of alternative fuels, the implementation of emission-reduction technologies, and the retrofitting of vessels for sustainability. Personnel are provided with hands-on training and practical experience, ensuring they can effectively operate and maintain green technologies.

Safety remains paramount in maritime operations, and education programs continue to prioritise safety training. However, these programs are evolving to incorporate eco-safety, integrating environmental awareness into safety protocols. This approach ensures that personnel not only uphold safety standards but also consider the ecological impact of their actions.

Vocational training and apprenticeships are essential to these programs, providing individuals with practical, on-the-job experience. These opportunities bridge the gap between theoretical knowledge and hands-on skills, preparing personnel for the demands of sustainable shipping practices.

Additionally, continuous professional development is emphasised, encouraging maritime personnel to stay current with evolving technologies, regulations, and best practices. Short courses, workshops, and certifications allow individuals to upgrade their skills and expertise continually.

Training and education programs for maritime personnel are essential for cultivating a skilled workforce capable of navigating the complexities of green shipping. By imparting knowledge, fostering hands-on experience, and emphasising safety and sustainability, these programs are instrumental in preparing maritime professionals for a future characterised by environmental responsibility and sustainability.

WORKFORCE DEVELOPMENT INITIATIVES

Workforce development initiatives within the maritime sector are instrumental in nurturing a skilled, adaptive, and forward-thinking workforce ready to embrace the challenges and opportunities of green shipping. These initiatives encompass a broad spectrum of strategies and programs to equip maritime professionals with the competencies and knowledge required for sustainable and environmentally responsible practices.

One pivotal aspect of these initiatives is the promotion of educational pathways that cater to the evolving needs of the industry. Maritime academies, universities, and vocational training centres collaborate with industry stakeholders to develop curricula that reflect the latest advancements in green shipping. This includes courses and degree programs focused on sustainability, environmental regulations, and clean technologies, ensuring that the workforce is well-versed in the principles of eco-conscious maritime practices.

Furthermore, apprenticeship programs and on-the-job training initiatives are critical workforce development components. These programs provide aspiring maritime professionals with hands-on experience under the guidance of seasoned mentors. They bridge the gap between theoretical knowledge and practical skills, nurturing a workforce that can effectively implement sustainable practices and green technologies in real-world scenarios.

Workforce development also emphasises diversity and inclusion, aiming to attract individuals from diverse backgrounds to maritime careers. Outreach programs, scholarships, and mentorship initiatives work in tandem to break down barriers and ensure that maritime opportunities are accessible and appealing to individuals of all genders, ethnicities, and backgrounds.

Continuous learning and professional development are hallmarks of workforce development initiatives. Maritime professionals are encouraged to engage in ongoing education and training, keeping them abreast of evolving technologies and regulations. Short courses, workshops, and certifications serve as avenues for skill enhancement and specialisation, fostering a culture of lifelong learning within the industry.

Lastly, industry partnerships and collaborations are central to these initiatives. Maritime companies, government bodies, educational institutions, and industry associations join forces to design and implement workforce development programs. These collaborative efforts ensure that the initiatives align with industry needs and facilitate the seamless integration of sustainability and environmental responsibility into maritime operations.

Workforce development initiatives in the maritime sector are multifaceted and dynamic to prepare a skilled workforce for the green shipping era. By emphasising education, practical training, diversity, continuous learning, and collaboration, these initiatives pave the way for a workforce that is not only capable but also committed to steering the industry towards a sustainable and environmentally responsible future.

Chapter 15

GLOBAL COLLABORATION FOR SUSTAINABLE SHIPPING

In an era defined by the imperative for sustainability and environmental responsibility, the maritime industry recognises that addressing the complex challenges of green shipping demands a collective and collaborative effort on a global scale. Chapter 15 delves into the critical domain of global collaboration for sustainable shipping, shedding light on the interconnected network of partnerships, agreements, and initiatives shaping the industry's eco-conscious future.

This chapter begins by unravelling the pivotal role international organisations play in facilitating global collaboration. Entities like the International Maritime Organisation (IMO) and the United Nations Framework Convention on Climate Change (UNFCCC) serve as catalysts for international cooperation, setting standards and regulations that govern emissions, ballast water management, and other environmental aspects of maritime operations.

Moreover, the chapter explores the significance of bilateral and multilateral agreements between nations. These agreements forge alliances aimed at reducing greenhouse gas emissions, curbing air and water pollution, and fostering eco-friendly practices in shipping. Examples include regional emissions control areas (ECAs) and agreements to combat illegal, unreported, and unregulated (IUU) fishing, which have wide-reaching implications for sustainable maritime activities.

Collaboration also extends to the private sector, where industry associations and alliances are taking centre stage. Organisations such as the Global Maritime Forum and the Getting to Zero Coalition unite maritime companies, research institutions, and advocacy groups to drive innovation and the adoption of clean technologies. These collaborations amplify the industry's commitment to sustainability and push the boundaries of green shipping practices.

Furthermore, this chapter delves into the role of technology-sharing initiatives in fostering sustainability. By sharing innovations, best practices, and technological advancements, countries and organisations accelerate the adoption of green technologies across the industry, creating a ripple effect of positive change.

Lastly, the chapter emphasises the importance of cross-sector collaboration. The maritime industry intersects with various sectors, including energy, logistics, and infrastructure. Collaborative efforts that span these sectors create synergies that amplify the impact of sustainability initiatives and drive the industry towards a more holistic and integrated approach to green shipping.

Chapter 15 serves as a beacon illuminating the indispensable role of global collaboration in steering the maritime industry towards a sustainable future. It underscores how partnerships, agreements, and shared commitments are pivotal in addressing the environmental challenges that define the era of green shipping, ultimately fostering a maritime sector that operates responsibly, efficiently, and harmoniously with the planet.

INTERNATIONAL INITIATIVES PROMOTING SUSTAINABLE SHIPPING

International initiatives promoting sustainable shipping are pivotal in shaping the maritime industry's commitment to environmental responsibility and eco-conscious practices. These initiatives serve as global platforms for collaboration, setting standards, and driving innovation towards a greener and more sustainable future for maritime activities. Several key international initiatives stand out:

INTERNATIONAL MARITIME ORGANISATION (IMO)

The IMO is at the forefront of global efforts to promote sustainable shipping. It has introduced a series of regulations, including the International Convention for the Control and Management of Ships' Ballast Water and Sediments and the MARPOL Annex VI, which sets limits on emissions of sulphur oxides (SOx) and nitrogen oxides (NOx). The IMO's initial strategy on greenhouse gas emissions aims to reduce emissions from international shipping by at least 50% by 2050 compared to 2008.

GLOBAL MARITIME ENERGY EFFICIENCY PARTNERSHIPS (GLOMEEP)

This initiative, led by the IMO, promotes energy-efficient shipping and reduces greenhouse gas emissions. GloMEEP provides technical assistance, capacity building, and support to developing countries to enhance their energy efficiency measures in the maritime sector.

GLOBAL INDUSTRY ALLIANCE (GIA) FOR MARINE BIOSAFETY

Addressing the pressing issue of invasive species in ballast water, the GIA brings together maritime industry stakeholders to develop innovative solutions for ballast water management and advance compliance with the Ballast Water Management Convention.

GLOBAL MARITIME FORUM (GMF)

The GMF is a private-sector-led initiative that fosters collaboration among industry leaders, policymakers, and other stakeholders. It focuses on driving innovation and sustainable practices in shipping, with initiatives like the "Getting to Zero Coalition," which aims to accelerate the adoption of zero-emission vessels.

UNITED NATIONS SUSTAINABLE DEVELOPMENT GOALS (SDGS)

While not exclusive to shipping, the SDGs provide a global framework for sustainability, including Goal 14, which focuses on conserving and sustainably using the oceans. The maritime industry is critical in achieving several SDGs, such as responsible consumption and production (Goal 12) and climate action (Goal 13).

PARIS AGREEMENT

Although not specific to shipping, the Paris Agreement under the UNFCCC calls for international efforts to limit global warming. The maritime industry, as a significant contributor to global emissions, is encouraged to align its actions with the objectives of the agreement.

SUSTAINABLE SHIPPING INITIATIVE (SSI)

While not a governmental initiative, the SSI is an international coalition of shipping companies and stakeholders committed to advancing sustainability in the industry. It focuses on various sustainability aspects, including emissions reduction, energy efficiency, and social responsibility.

These international initiatives showcase the collaborative spirit and shared commitment of governments, industry players, and organisations to address the environmental challenges posed by maritime shipping. By setting targets, developing regulations, and promoting sustainable practices, these initiatives drive the industry towards a more environmentally responsible and sustainable future.

COLLABORATIVE EFFORTS AMONG NATIONS, ORGANISATIONS, AND INDUSTRIES

Collaborative efforts among nations, organisations, and industries are pivotal in addressing global challenges, including sustainability and environmental responsibility in maritime shipping. These collaborative endeavours foster innovation, knowledge sharing, and collective action to tackle complex issues. Several noteworthy examples illustrate the power of such collaborations:

INTERNATIONAL MARITIME ORGANISATION (IMO)

The IMO, a specialised agency of the United Nations, exemplifies international collaboration. Member nations come together to develop and implement regulations governing shipping activities, including emissions reduction, ballast water management, and safety standards. The IMO's conventions, such as MARPOL and SOLAS, serve as global frameworks for responsible maritime operations.

GLOBAL MARITIME FORUM (GMF)

The GMF brings together stakeholders from across the maritime industry, including shipping companies, policymakers, and NGOs. Through collaborative initiatives like the "Getting to Zero Coalition," the GMF aims to accelerate the transition to zero-emission vessels. This private-sector-led effort highlights the power of industry collaboration to drive sustainable innovation.

GLOBAL INDUSTRY ALLIANCE (GIA) FOR MARINE BIOSAFETY

The GIA is an industry-led partnership working to address invasive species in ballast water. Shipping companies, technology providers, and organisations collaborate to develop effective ballast water management solutions and support compliance with international regulations.

REGIONAL EMISSIONS CONTROL AREAS (ECAS)

These regional agreements involve multiple nations establishing stricter emissions standards for vessels operating within defined geographical areas. For instance, the North American ECA and the Baltic Sea ECA aim to reduce air pollutant emissions, promoting cleaner shipping practices in these regions.

PARTNERSHIPS FOR SUSTAINABLE PORTS

Ports are integral to maritime shipping, and collaborative efforts are essential to promote sustainability. Various organisations, including port authorities, environmental groups, and shipping companies, collaborate on initiatives to reduce port emissions, enhance energy efficiency, and implement eco-friendly practices.

GREEN SHIPPING ALLIANCES

Shipping companies often form alliances and partnerships to invest in research and development of green technologies collectively. These alliances pool resources and expertise to accelerate the adoption of clean propulsion systems, energy-efficient designs, and sustainable practices across their fleets.

UNITED NATIONS SUSTAINABLE DEVELOPMENT GOALS (SDGS)

Collaboration across nations, industries, and organisations is fundamental to achieving the SDGs. The maritime sector contributes to several goals, including responsible consumption and production, climate action, and life below water. By aligning their efforts with the SDGs, stakeholders work together to address broader sustainability challenges.

RESEARCH AND INNOVATION COLLABORATIONS

Industry players, research institutions, and governments collaborate on projects focused on sustainable shipping solutions. These partnerships drive innovation in alternative fuels, energy-efficient vessel designs, and emissions-reduction technologies.

Collaborative efforts among nations, organisations, and industries demonstrate the capacity for collective action in addressing the environmental challenges of maritime shipping. These collaborations leverage diverse expertise, resources, and perspectives to drive innovation and promote sustainable practices in an industry vital to global trade and sustainability.

ACHIEVING A UNITED FRONT FOR GREEN MARITIME PRACTICES

Achieving a united front for green maritime practices is imperative in pursuing a sustainable and environmentally responsible future for the industry. This unity, forged through collaboration among nations, organisations, and industries, is not just a desirable outcome but a fundamental necessity in addressing the complex challenges posed by maritime shipping.

First and foremost, a united front signifies the recognition of shared responsibility. Maritime activities, by their nature, transcend borders and jurisdictions. They affect the global environment, oceans, and communities. Acknowledging this shared impact fosters a collective duty to protect the planet and its ecosystems.

A united front is also about aligning on common goals and objectives. Nations, organisations, and industries must converge around a clear vision of sustainable shipping. This includes reducing emissions, minimising environmental impact, and adopting eco-friendly technologies. A common purpose provides a roadmap for coordinated action.

Collaboration fosters the exchange of knowledge and best practices. The maritime industry is diverse and multifaceted, with various stakeholders possessing unique expertise. By coming together, these stakeholders can pool their insights, innovations, and experiences, accelerating progress toward green shipping practices.

Furthermore, a united front enhances regulatory harmonisation. When nations agree on international regulations and standards, it eliminates discrepancies and ensures a level playing field for all. This consistency not only simplifies compliance but also encourages innovation as stakeholders can focus their efforts on meeting common standards.

Collective action amplifies the industry's voice. By presenting a unified front, maritime stakeholders can engage more effectively with policymakers, advocating for regulations that support sustainability while balancing economic viability. This collaborative advocacy strengthens the industry's position and influence.

Achieving a united front for green maritime practices transcends mere cooperation; it embodies a commitment to a shared destiny. It represents the industry's dedication to environmental stewardship, technological advancement, and responsible operations. Together, nations, organisations, and industries can navigate the challenges of sustainable shipping, steering the maritime sector toward a future where ecological responsibility and economic vitality coexist harmoniously.

Chapter 16

FUTURE TRENDS AND ECHNOLOGICAL INNOVATIONS

The maritime industry is on the cusp of a transformative journey, navigating towards a future characterised by sustainability, efficiency, and technological advancement. Chapter 16 embarks on an exploration of the future trends and technological innovations that will redefine the landscape of maritime shipping in the coming years.

This chapter begins by delving into the acceleration of decarbonisation efforts. It scrutinises adopting alternative fuels such as hydrogen, ammonia, and biofuels alongside developing zero-emission vessels. These technologies are poised to revolutionise the industry by significantly reducing greenhouse gas emissions and ushering in a new era of green shipping.

Moreover, the chapter ventures into the domain of autonomous shipping. It unveils the advancements in artificial intelligence, machine learning, and sensor technologies, propelling vessels towards autonomy. The implications of autonomous vessels, including enhanced safety, operational efficiency, and reduced labour costs, are thoroughly examined.

The future of maritime logistics is another focal point as the industry witnesses the integration of blockchain, IoT, and big data analytics. These technologies promise to optimise supply chain operations, enhance cargo tracking, and reduce inefficiencies, ultimately streamlining maritime logistics on a global scale.

Additionally, this chapter explores the potential of electrification in maritime transport. The electrification of short-sea shipping and the development of electric ferry system's showcase how electrified propulsion systems can contribute to cleaner and quieter maritime operations, particularly in coastal regions.

Furthermore, the emergence of 3D printing and additive manufacturing in shipbuilding is unveiled. These innovations revolutionise vessel construction by enabling rapid prototyping, customised components, and reduced material waste.

The maritime industry's commitment to circular economy principles is also illuminated in this chapter. Sustainable ship recycling practices and developing ships designed for end-of-life recycling are poised to reshape how the industry approaches vessel decommissioning.

Lastly, the chapter peers into the future of cybersecurity in maritime operations. With the growing dependence on digital systems and connectivity, safeguarding vessels from cyber threats is becoming increasingly critical, necessitating robust cybersecurity measures and strategies.

EMERGING TECHNOLOGIES AND TRENDS IN RENEWABLE MARITIME ENERGY

Emerging technologies and trends in renewable maritime energy are steering the industry towards a more sustainable and environmentally responsible future. One of the most notable trends is the increasing adoption of alternative fuels and propulsion systems. Hydrogen and ammonia are gaining prominence as green fuels for vessels, offering zero-emission propulsion options. These fuels are produced through renewable energy sources, addressing the maritime sector's commitment to reducing greenhouse gas emissions significantly.

Another significant trend is the development of zero-emission vessels. Electric and hybrid-electric ships are becoming more prevalent, particularly in the ferry and short-sea shipping sectors. These vessels utilise advanced battery technologies and electric propulsion systems to operate silently and with minimal environmental impact. Furthermore, integrating renewable energy sources, such as wind and solar power, enhances vessel efficiency and reduces reliance on traditional fossil fuels.

Autonomous shipping is poised to revolutionise the industry. With advancements in artificial intelligence and automation, autonomous vessels are becoming a reality. These ships offer improved safety, increased operational efficiency, and reduced labour costs. The maritime sector is witnessing pilot projects and trials of autonomous ships, heralding a new era of crewless maritime transport.

Digitalisation and data analytics are transforming maritime operations. The use of IoT sensors, blockchain, and big data analytics is optimising vessel performance, route planning, and cargo tracking. These technologies enhance decision-making processes, reduce fuel consumption, and minimise inefficiencies, contributing to a more sustainable and cost-effective maritime industry.

Sustainable ship design and materials are gaining traction. Shipbuilders are exploring eco-friendly materials, innovative hull designs, and lightweight construction techniques to enhance vessel efficiency and reduce environmental impact. Ships designed with a focus on sustainability offer better fuel economy and lower emissions throughout their lifecycle.

Lastly, circular economy principles are shaping ship recycling practices. Sustainable ship recycling facilities are emerging, focusing on environmentally responsible decommissioning methods. The industry is also witnessing the design of ships with recycling in mind, making it easier to dismantle and repurpose vessels at the end of their operational life.

Emerging technologies and trends in renewable maritime energy are ushering in a transformative era for the industry. With a focus on alternative fuels, zero-emission vessels, autonomous shipping, digitalisation, sustainable design, and responsible recycling, the maritime sector is on the path to a greener and more efficient future, aligning with global efforts to combat climate change and reduce environmental impact.

PREDICTIONS FOR THE FUTURE OF GREEN SHIPPING

Predicting the future of green shipping involves envisioning a maritime industry increasingly focused on sustainability, environmental responsibility, and technological innovation. Several key predictions for the future of green shipping include:

- **Widespread Adoption of Zero-Emission Vessels:** The maritime industry will witness a significant increase in the adoption of zero-emission vessels, including electric, hydrogen, and ammonia-powered ships. These vessels will become commonplace, particularly in short-sea shipping and coastal transport, substantially reducing greenhouse gas emissions.
- **Advanced Autonomous Shipping:** Autonomous shipping will evolve from experimental phases to practical implementation. Maritime transport will see the deployment of autonomous vessels for various purposes, ranging from cargo transport to maritime surveillance. These autonomous ships will not only enhance safety but also improve operational efficiency.
- **Hybrid Propulsion Systems:** Hybrid propulsion systems, combining traditional fuels with electric or hydrogen power, will become standard in the industry. These systems will offer flexibility and emissions reductions, allowing vessels to transition gradually to cleaner energy sources.
- **Green Port Initiatives:** Ports worldwide will embrace sustainability initiatives, incorporating renewable energy sources, efficient cargo handling technologies, and eco-friendly infrastructure. Ports will become hubs for clean energy production and distribution, facilitating the integration of renewable energy into maritime operations.
- **Circular Economy Principles in Ship Design:** Vessels will be designed with circular economy principles in mind, ensuring they are easily recyclable and environmentally friendly at the end of their operational life. Sustainable shipbuilding materials and construction techniques will become the norm.
- **Digitalisation and Data-Driven Efficiency:** The maritime industry will extensively leverage digitalisation, IoT, and data analytics to optimise operations. Smart ships will continuously monitor and adjust their performance, reducing fuel consumption, emissions, and operational costs.
- **International Collaboration on Sustainability:** Global collaboration and agreements on emissions reduction and environmental protection will continue to strengthen. More nations will join forces to develop and enforce international regulations, creating a level playing field for sustainable maritime practices.
- **Renewable Energy Integration:** Maritime vessels will increasingly integrate renewable energy sources, such as wind and solar power, into their onboard systems. These sources will supplement traditional power generation, reducing reliance on fossil fuels during voyages.

- **Green Finance and Incentives:** Financial institutions and governments will provide incentives and funding for sustainable shipping projects. Green finance mechanisms will support the transition to cleaner technologies and practices, making sustainable investments more attractive.
- **Enhanced Environmental Monitoring:** Real-time environmental monitoring systems will become standard on vessels, enabling crews to assess their environmental impact and adjust accordingly. This proactive approach will lead to better compliance with environmental regulations.

The future of green shipping promises a maritime industry that prioritises sustainability, embraces innovative technologies, and works globally to reduce its environmental footprint. These predictions reflect a growing commitment to environmental responsibility and a determination to navigate the industry towards a more sustainable and eco-conscious future.

THE ROLE OF INNOVATION IN SHAPING THE INDUSTRY

Innovation is pivotal in shaping the maritime industry, driving positive changes, and steering it towards a more sustainable, efficient, and environmentally responsible future. Here are several key aspects of innovation in the industry:

TECHNOLOGICAL ADVANCEMENTS

Technological innovation is at the forefront of reshaping the maritime sector. Advances in propulsion systems, materials science, and ship design are transforming vessels into cleaner and more efficient machines. For example, developing alternative fuels and hybrid propulsion systems reduces emissions and improves fuel efficiency, aligning with global sustainability goals.

AUTONOMOUS SHIPPING

Innovation in automation, artificial intelligence, and navigation systems fosters the emergence of autonomous shipping. Crewless vessels promise enhanced safety, reduced human error, and optimised route planning. The integration of autonomous technologies will revolutionise the way maritime operations are conducted, leading to increased efficiency and cost savings.

DIGITALISATION AND DATA ANALYTICS

The maritime industry is undergoing a digital transformation. IoT sensors, big data analytics, and blockchain technology enhance data-driven decision-making. Real-time monitoring of vessel performance, cargo tracking, and supply chain optimisation benefit from digital innovations, leading to improved operational efficiency and reduced environmental impact.

CLEAN ENERGY INTEGRATION

Innovations in renewable energy integration are reshaping the industry's energy landscape. Wind-assist and solar-assist technologies are being incorporated into vessel designs to harness clean energy sources. These innovations reduce reliance on fossil fuels, lower emissions, and contribute to a greener maritime sector.

ECO-FRIENDLY SHIP MATERIALS

Innovations in shipbuilding materials are promoting sustainability. The development of lightweight and eco-friendly materials is reducing vessel weight, improving fuel efficiency, and enhancing overall performance. Sustainable ship designs also focus on minimising environmental impact throughout a vessel's lifecycle.

CIRCULAR ECONOMY PRINCIPLES

Innovations in ship design and recycling are embracing circular economy principles. Ships are being designed with recyclability, facilitating responsible end-of-life disposal and reducing waste. Sustainable ship recycling practices are emerging, ensuring that vessels are dismantled in an environmentally friendly manner.

GREEN PORT INFRASTRUCTURE

Ports are adopting innovative solutions to reduce their environmental footprint. Investments in eco-friendly port infrastructure, such as shore power and renewable energy sources, enable vessels to operate more sustainably while in port. This innovation enhances the overall sustainability of maritime logistics.

ENVIRONMENTAL MONITORING TECHNOLOGIES

Innovations in environmental monitoring technologies enable real-time assessment of emissions and water quality. These monitoring systems assist vessels in complying with environmental regulations and provide valuable data for optimising fuel consumption and emissions reduction strategies.

SAFETY AND SECURITY INNOVATIONS

The maritime industry continuously innovates in safety and security measures. Advanced communication systems, navigation aids, and emergency response technologies improve vessel safety. Innovations in cybersecurity are critical to safeguarding digital systems from potential threats.

SUSTAINABLE SHIP FINANCE

Innovations in financial instruments, such as green bonds and sustainability-linked loans, support the maritime industry's transition to sustainability. These financial mechanisms encourage investments in eco-friendly technologies and practices, aligning financial incentives with environmental responsibility.

Innovation is a driving force that shapes the maritime industry by introducing new technologies, materials, and practices that enhance sustainability, safety, and efficiency. These innovations benefit the industry and contribute to global efforts to combat climate change and protect marine ecosystems.

Chapter 17

ENVIRONMENTAL REPORTING AND ACCOUNTABILITY

In an era where environmental responsibility is paramount, the maritime industry is undergoing a profound transformation in how it reports and holds itself accountable for its environmental impact. Chapter 17 delves into the critical domain of environmental reporting and accountability within the maritime sector, shedding light on the mechanisms, frameworks, and initiatives shaping this crucial aspect of the industry.

This chapter begins by examining the significance of transparent environmental reporting. It underscores how accurate and comprehensive reporting is the cornerstone of accountability, enabling stakeholders to assess and monitor the industry's adherence to environmental regulations and sustainability goals.

Moreover, the chapter explores the emergence of international and national regulations mandating environmental reporting. It delves into key regulations such as the International Maritime Organisation's (IMO) Data Collection System (DCS) and the European Union's Monitoring, Reporting, and Verification (MRV) scheme. These regulations necessitate vessel operators to report various environmental parameters, including fuel consumption, emissions, and energy efficiency indicators.

The chapter also unveils the role of technology in facilitating environmental reporting. Innovative solutions, such as onboard monitoring systems and digital reporting platforms, simplify data collection and transmission. These technologies enhance the accuracy and timeliness of reporting, empowering the industry to meet its compliance obligations effectively.

Furthermore, the chapter delves into the concept of sustainability reporting. It emphasises how maritime companies increasingly integrate environmental, social, and governance (ESG) factors into their reporting frameworks. Sustainability reports offer a holistic view of a company's commitment to responsible operations, covering emissions reduction, community engagement, and ethical business practices.

Environmental reporting is closely tied to corporate social responsibility (CSR) and stakeholder engagement. The chapter underscores how maritime companies engage with stakeholders, including customers, investors, and communities, through transparent reporting. These efforts build trust and align business goals with societal and environmental expectations.

The chapter explores the future of environmental reporting and accountability in the maritime industry. It highlights the potential for increased collaboration, data standardisation, and alignment with international sustainability frameworks, such as the United Nations Sustainable Development Goals (SDGs). It envisions an industry that reports its environmental impact and proactively seeks opportunities for improvement and innovation.

REPORTING REQUIREMENTS FOR ENVIRONMENTAL PERFORMANCE

Reporting requirements for environmental performance in the maritime industry are becoming increasingly stringent and standardised, reflecting the industry's commitment to sustainability and accountability. These requirements encompass various aspects of a vessel's environmental impact and are driven by international and national regulations. Key reporting elements include:

EMISSIONS MONITORING AND REPORTING

Emissions Monitoring and Reporting play a pivotal role in the maritime industry's efforts to enhance environmental sustainability and reduce its carbon footprint. Vessel operators are required to engage in meticulous monitoring and reporting of various emissions, including greenhouse gases (GHGs) such as carbon dioxide (CO_2), sulphur oxides (SOx), nitrogen oxides (NOx), and particulate matter (PM). These efforts are driven by international regulations, most notably the International Maritime Organisation's (IMO) Data Collection System (DCS), which mandates the comprehensive tracking of ship emissions. This rigorous reporting ensures compliance with international standards and provides a crucial foundation for reducing emissions and improving overall vessel efficiency.

Given its significant role in global trade and transportation, the maritime industry recognises the urgent need to address its environmental impact. GHGs, in particular, are a major concern as they contribute to climate change and air pollution. Emissions monitoring is the first step in understanding the magnitude of this impact, and accurate reporting is essential to provide transparency and accountability.

The IMO's DCS, introduced to monitor ship emissions, requires vessels to gather data on various emission sources, including the main engines, auxiliary engines, and boilers. This data encompasses fuel consumption, distances travelled, and operational hours, providing a comprehensive view of emissions produced during voyages. Vessel operators must submit this data to competent authorities for assessment.

Beyond regulatory compliance, emissions monitoring and reporting serve broader purposes. They facilitate the maritime industry's transition towards sustainability by offering insights into fuel efficiency and emission reduction opportunities. Vessel operators can identify areas where improvements can be made, such as adopting cleaner fuels, optimising routes, or enhancing onboard technologies to reduce emissions.

Furthermore, emissions reporting supports developing and enforcing international and national regulations to curb emissions from the maritime sector. By providing a robust emissions data foundation, authorities can accurately assess the industry's environmental impact and implement measures to reduce it effectively.

Emissions monitoring and reporting are integral to the maritime industry's commitment to environmental responsibility. By meticulously tracking and reporting emissions, vessel operators comply with international standards and contribute to a cleaner, more sustainable future for the industry. These efforts are essential steps towards reducing emissions, improving vessel efficiency, and addressing the pressing challenges of climate change and air quality in maritime shipping.

FUEL CONSUMPTION DATA

Accurate reporting of fuel consumption data holds a pivotal role in the maritime industry's commitment to environmental performance assessment and sustainability. Vessel operators are responsible for meticulously recording and reporting fuel consumption data, encompassing different fuel types and consumption rates throughout various voyage phases. This invaluable information serves multiple essential purposes, including calculating crucial energy efficiency indicators like the Energy Efficiency Existing Ship Index (EEXI), all aimed at optimising fuel usage and reducing carbon emissions. These reporting practices align with the broader industry-wide efforts to combat climate change and foster sustainable shipping practices.

Fuel consumption data is a cornerstone in the maritime sector's ongoing efforts to enhance its environmental performance. It forms the basis for evaluating a vessel's energy efficiency and carbon emissions. This data takes into account various factors, such as the type of fuel used (e.g., heavy fuel oil, diesel, LNG), fuel consumption rates during different operational phases (e.g., cruising, idling, manoeuvring), and the distances covered during voyages.

One of the primary applications of this data is the calculation of the Energy Efficiency Existing Ship Index (EEXI), which is a critical tool for assessing a vessel's compliance with international regulations aimed at reducing carbon intensity. Vessel operators must ensure their ships meet EEXI requirements to align with the industry's goals for emission reduction.

Beyond regulatory compliance, fuel consumption data reporting offers numerous benefits. It gives vessel operators insights into their fleet's performance and identifies opportunities for optimising fuel usage. By analysing this data, operators can implement measures to enhance fuel efficiency, reduce operational costs, and minimise the environmental impact of their operations.

Additionally, transparent and accurate fuel consumption reporting supports the maritime industry's broader sustainability objectives. It allows stakeholders, including regulators, customers, and the public, to assess the industry's progress in reducing greenhouse gas emissions and adopting cleaner fuels and technologies.

The accurate reporting of fuel consumption data is an essential practice within the maritime industry, driven by both regulatory mandates and the industry's commitment to sustainability. This data is a critical tool for evaluating energy efficiency, complying with international regulations like the EEXI, and identifying opportunities for fuel optimisation. Ultimately, it contributes to the industry's collective efforts to combat climate change and promote sustainable shipping practices.

ENERGY EFFICIENCY INDICATORS

Energy Efficiency Indicators are integral to the maritime industry's commitment to environmental responsibility and sustainability. These indicators, such as the Energy Efficiency Operational Indicator (EEOI), provide valuable insights into a vessel's operational performance and environmental impact. By continuously measuring and reporting EEOI data, maritime companies can monitor their vessels' efficiency trends, establish performance benchmarks, and implement strategies to enhance energy efficiency while concurrently reducing emissions.

The Energy Efficiency Operational Indicator (EEOI) is a crucial metric for assessing the energy efficiency of vessels. It relates a vessel's carbon emissions to its transport work, providing a comprehensive view of how efficiently a ship operates regarding energy consumption and environmental impact. The formula for calculating EEOI typically considers factors such as fuel consumption, distance travelled, and the quantity of cargo transported.

Continuous measurement and reporting of EEOI data offer several notable advantages to maritime companies:

- **Performance Monitoring:** EEOI data allows companies to monitor their vessels' energy efficiency in real-time and over extended periods. This data enables operators to identify efficiency trends and evaluate the impact of various operational factors on energy consumption.
- **Benchmarking:** Establishing EEOI benchmarks allows maritime companies to set clear performance goals and compare the energy efficiency of different vessels within their fleet. Benchmarking can encourage healthy competition among vessels and drive improvements.
- **Efficiency Strategies:** Armed with EEOI data, operators can identify areas where energy efficiency can be enhanced. This may involve adjusting vessel speeds, optimising routes, adopting cleaner fuels, or investing in energy-saving technologies.
- **Emission Reduction:** Enhancing energy efficiency, as measured by EEOI, leads to reduced carbon emissions per unit of cargo transported. This aligns with global efforts to mitigate climate change and comply with emission reduction targets.
- **Regulatory Compliance:** EEOI reporting is a requirement under various international regulations, including the Energy Efficiency Existing Ship Index (EEXI) introduced by the International Maritime Organisation (IMO). Compliance with these regulations is essential for vessels operating within global maritime trade.

Energy efficiency indicators, particularly the Energy Efficiency Operational Indicator (EEOI), play a pivotal role in the maritime industry's commitment to reducing emissions and enhancing sustainability. By measuring and reporting EEOI data, maritime companies gain actionable insights into vessel efficiency, enabling them to set goals, implement strategies, and make informed decisions that ultimately contribute to more energy-efficient and environmentally responsible maritime operations. These indicators are critical in the industry's ongoing efforts to navigate towards a cleaner and more sustainable future.

BALLAST WATER MANAGEMENT REPORTING

Ballast Water Management Reporting is critical to the maritime industry's commitment to environmental protection and sustainability. It addresses ecological challenges associated with ballast water discharge, which can inadvertently introduce invasive species into new ecosystems. In response to these challenges, reporting requirements have been established to demand the documentation of ballast water management practices. These reports encompass ballast water treatment systems, discharge volumes, and compliance with international standards, notably the Ballast Water Management Convention. Accurate reporting is indispensable for safeguarding marine biodiversity and ensuring compliance with environmental regulations.

Ballast water is essential for maintaining the stability and safety of vessels during transit, but it can unintentionally carry aquatic species from one location to another. When discharged into new ecosystems, these non-native species can disrupt the balance of local ecosystems, harm native species, and damage biodiversity.

The Ballast Water Management Convention, adopted by the International Maritime Organisation (IMO), establishes clear guidelines and standards for managing and treating ballast water to prevent the spread of invasive species. Vessel operators must document and report their ballast water management practices to demonstrate compliance with these international regulations.

Accurate and transparent reporting of ballast water management practices serves several important purposes:

- **Environmental Protection:** Reporting ensures that vessels implement proper ballast water management procedures, including using ballast water treatment systems. This contributes to the protection of marine biodiversity and the prevention of invasive species introduction.
- **Regulatory Compliance:** Vessel operators must comply with international regulations, such as the Ballast Water Management Convention, which sets clear standards for ballast water management. Compliance reporting is essential to demonstrate adherence to these standards.
- **Data Collection:** By documenting ballast water management practices, authorities can collect valuable data on the implementation of treatment technologies, discharge volumes, and the effectiveness of measures in preventing invasive species' transfer.
- **Transparency:** Transparency in reporting allows for scrutiny by regulatory bodies and stakeholders, promoting accountability and adherence to best practices.
- **Scientific Research:** Accurate reporting can aid scientific research into the impact of ballast water discharge on ecosystems and the effectiveness of treatment methods.

Ballast water management reporting is essential to the maritime industry's commitment to environmental stewardship. By accurately documenting and reporting their ballast water management practices, vessel operators play a crucial role in preventing the spread of invasive species, protecting marine ecosystems, and ensuring compliance with international environmental regulations. This reporting practice aligns with broader efforts to promote sustainable and responsible maritime operations.

WASTE MANAGEMENT AND DISPOSAL RECORDS

Environmental performance reporting also encompasses waste management and disposal records. Vessel operators are obliged to maintain records of waste generation, handling, and disposal practices in accordance with MARPOL Annex V regulations. This reporting helps prevent marine pollution and demonstrates a commitment to responsible waste management, which is integral to sustainable maritime operations.

These reporting requirements underscore the maritime industry's dedication to environmental responsibility and accountability. By meticulously monitoring and reporting emissions, fuel consumption, energy efficiency, ballast water management, and waste disposal practices, vessel operators contribute to global efforts to reduce the industry's ecological footprint and foster a more sustainable future for maritime shipping.

TRANSPARENCY AND ACCOUNTABILITY IN SUSTAINABLE SHIPPING

Transparency and accountability are the cornerstones of sustainable shipping, underpinning the maritime industry's commitment to responsible practices and environmental stewardship. These principles ensure the industry operates with openness and responsibility, fostering stakeholder trust and advancing sustainability goals.

Transparency in sustainable shipping involves the clear and accessible disclosure of environmental data and practices. This includes reporting on emissions, fuel consumption, energy efficiency, and compliance with environmental regulations. Vessel operators and shipping companies are increasingly expected to provide detailed information about their environmental performance, allowing stakeholders to evaluate their impact and adherence to sustainability objectives.

Accountability, on the other hand, goes hand in hand with transparency. It entails taking responsibility for one's actions and their consequences. In sustainable shipping, accountability means acknowledging the environmental impact of maritime operations and taking proactive measures to mitigate it. This includes investing in cleaner technologies, adopting alternative fuels, and adhering to international and national regulations to reduce emissions and improve environmental performance.

Transparency and accountability drive the maritime industry toward a more sustainable and responsible future. They enable stakeholders, including governments, investors, customers, and the public, to assess the industry's progress in reducing its environmental footprint. Moreover, these principles encourage continuous improvement, innovation, and a collective commitment to address the complex challenges posed by shipping activities on a global scale.

Transparency and accountability are ethical imperatives and essential components of sustainable shipping. They empower the industry to make informed decisions, track progress, and fulfil its environmental responsibilities. As the maritime sector navigates toward a greener and more sustainable future, these principles will remain fundamental to its success in balancing economic viability with ecological responsibility.

BENEFITS OF ENVIRONMENTALLY RESPONSIBLE PRACTICES

Embracing environmentally responsible practices in the maritime industry yields many benefits beyond compliance with regulations. These practices, which prioritise sustainability and reduce the industry's environmental footprint, have numerous advantages, encompassing economic, environmental, and social dimensions.

1. **ECONOMIC VIABILITY**:

Economic viability is a fundamental consideration in the maritime industry and is increasingly intertwined with environmentally responsible practices. Adopting these practices can significantly enhance the economic sustainability of maritime operations. One of the primary ways this occurs is through the reduction of fuel consumption achieved by improving energy efficiency. When vessels become more fuel-efficient, they reduce their environmental footprint and realise substantial cost savings. Less fuel consumption means lower operational expenses, which can have a profound impact on the bottom line of maritime companies.

Furthermore, investments in green technologies and alternative fuels can lead to long-term financial benefits. In an industry often affected by the volatility of fossil fuel prices, transitioning to cleaner and more sustainable energy sources can provide stability and predictability. For instance, adopting liquefied natural gas (LNG) or other low-emission fuels can hedge against the fluctuations in traditional fuel prices, offering a more consistent and controlled cost structure over time.

Additionally, green technologies can lead to innovations that result in economic advantages. Research and development efforts in clean propulsion technologies, energy-efficient systems, and renewable energy integration can drive industry-wide innovation. Companies that invest in such technologies contribute to sustainability and position themselves as leaders in the field, potentially attracting environmentally conscious customers and investors.

Economic viability and environmental responsibility in maritime operations are not mutually exclusive; they are interdependent. By embracing environmentally responsible practices, maritime companies can reduce fuel consumption, resulting in immediate cost savings. Furthermore, long-term investments in green technologies and alternative fuels offer financial stability and the potential for competitive advantages in an industry marked by economic fluctuations. Ultimately, the economic benefits of sustainable practices in maritime shipping extend beyond mere cost savings, contributing to a more resilient and prosperous future for the industry.

1. **REGULATORY COMPLIANCE**

Regulatory compliance has become an essential consideration for maritime companies in today's global landscape, where stringent environmental regulations are increasingly enforced. Embracing responsible practices aligns with these regulations and helps maritime companies avoid costly fines and penalties associated with non-compliance. Moreover, compliance is a gateway to markets prioritising sustainable shipping, creating additional economic advantages.

The maritime industry operates within a complex web of international and national regulations aimed at mitigating its environmental impact. Regulations, such as those set forth by the International Maritime Organisation (IMO), target maritime operations, including emissions reduction, ballast water management, and vessel efficiency. Non-compliance with these regulations can result in significant financial repercussions, including fines, penalties, and potential damage to a company's reputation.

By embracing responsible practices, maritime companies can ensure they meet or exceed these regulatory requirements. For example, adopting energy-efficient technologies, utilising cleaner fuels, and implementing ballast water treatment systems demonstrate a commitment to environmental compliance. These practices help avoid regulatory penalties and position companies as responsible and environmentally conscious operators.

Furthermore, regulatory compliance opens doors to new markets and business opportunities. Many regions and industries prioritise sustainable shipping practices, and Favor companies committed to environmental responsibility. Access to these markets can be critical for expanding a company's customer base and diversifying its revenue streams. It also aligns with the global shift towards sustainability, which can enhance a company's reputation and attractiveness to environmentally conscious customers and investors.

Regulatory compliance is not just a legal requirement but a strategic imperative for maritime companies. Embracing responsible practices ensures adherence to stringent environmental regulations, avoiding the financial risks associated with non-compliance. Additionally, compliance enables access to markets that value sustainability, positioning companies for long-term economic viability and success in an evolving and environmentally conscious global landscape.

1. **ENHANCED REPUTATION**

In today's environmentally conscious world, a commitment to environmental responsibility can be a powerful catalyst for enhancing a company's reputation. Demonstrating a proactive stance toward sustainability resonates strongly with customers, investors, and stakeholders who increasingly prioritise environmentally responsible practices in their decision-making processes. Companies that visibly invest in reducing their environmental impact and adopting green technologies can earn trust and goodwill from these key audiences.

A positive reputation built on sustainability opens doors to new business opportunities and strengthens a company's market competitiveness. Customers are likelier to choose products or services from companies known for their eco-friendly practices, particularly in sectors where sustainability is a distinguishing factor. This enhanced reputation can increase customer loyalty, a larger customer base, and a stronger brand presence.

Furthermore, investors are increasingly factoring environmental, social, and governance (ESG) criteria into their investment decisions, making companies with robust sustainability initiatives more attractive prospects. As a result, enhancing reputation through environmental responsibility is not just a goodwill gesture but a strategic investment that can drive growth and long-term success in an evolving market landscape.

1. **REDUCED ENVIRONMENTAL IMPACT**

Embracing environmentally responsible practices within the maritime industry promises to reduce its environmental footprint significantly. This reduction encompasses lower emissions, reduced pollution, and minimised habitat disruption, all yield substantial benefits for marine ecosystems and coastal communities. These collective efforts contribute to immediate environmental improvements and underpin the long-term sustainability of the industry and the ecosystems it operates within.

One of the primary environmental benefits of responsible maritime practices is reducing emissions, including greenhouse gases and air pollutants. By optimising vessel efficiency, adopting cleaner fuels, and implementing emission reduction technologies, the industry can substantially lower its carbon footprint. This aligns with global efforts to combat climate change and mitigate its consequences, such as sea-level rise and ocean acidification. Reduced emissions also result in improved air quality, benefiting not only marine life but also the health and well-being of coastal communities.

Additionally, environmentally responsible practices help curtail pollution in marine environments. Measures such as ballast water treatment systems and strict adherence to waste disposal regulations prevent the release of harmful substances into oceans and seas. This contributes to cleaner waters, healthier ecosystems, and the preservation of biodiversity. Reduced habitat disruption, achieved by minimising the environmental impact of shipping operations, ensures that marine ecosystems can thrive and regenerate naturally. Ultimately, these combined efforts promote harmonious coexistence between maritime activities and the fragile ecosystems in which they intersect, safeguarding the long-term environmental sustainability of both.

1. **RESOURCE CONSERVATION**

Embracing responsible practices within the maritime industry is pivotal in promoting resource conservation, a fundamental pillar of sustainable operations. These practices encompass a range of strategies that yield multifaceted benefits, including the preservation of finite fossil fuel resources, sustainable ship design, and resource-efficient recycling processes.

One of the most significant contributions to resource conservation is the reduction in fuel consumption achieved through improved energy efficiency. By optimising vessel operations, embracing eco-friendly propulsion technologies, and adopting smart route planning, maritime companies can significantly lower their fuel consumption. This translates into lower greenhouse gas emissions and conserves finite fossil fuel resources, ensuring their availability for future generations. Preserving these resources is vital in a global energy landscape with increasing demand and concerns over energy security.

Sustainable ship design also plays a pivotal role in resource conservation. Maritime companies that invest in eco-friendly vessel designs prioritise resource efficiency, reducing the demand for raw materials. Innovative shipbuilding techniques, recycled materials, and modular designs that enable easy component replacement all minimise the industry's environmental footprint. This approach conserves resources and aligns with circular economy principles, where materials are reused, refurbished, or recycled to extend their lifecycle.

Moreover, responsible practices extend to the recycling and disposal of maritime assets, including ships, at the end of their operational life. Implementing responsible recycling practices ensures that valuable materials are reclaimed and repurposed, minimising waste and further contributing to resource efficiency.

Resource conservation is at the heart of environmentally responsible maritime practices. By reducing fuel consumption, embracing sustainable ship design, and implementing resource-efficient recycling processes, the industry reduces its environmental impact and secures a more sustainable and resource-responsible future. These practices demonstrate a commitment to stewardship of the Earth's finite resources and contribute to the overall sustainability of the maritime sector.

1. **HEALTH AND SAFETY**

The maritime industry's pursuit of improved environmental practices goes hand in hand with fostering a safer working environment for its personnel. As responsible practices are embraced, a range of safety measures is implemented, reducing exposure to hazardous substances and minimising pollution risks. These collective efforts contribute significantly to better health and safety outcomes for both crew members and the communities in which maritime operations take place.

One key aspect of improved safety in the maritime sector is the implementation of stringent safety protocols. As environmental regulations become more stringent, maritime companies are compelled to adopt comprehensive safety measures. These protocols encompass the proper handling and storage of fuels, chemicals, and hazardous materials. The meticulous management of these substances reduces the risk of accidents, spills, and exposure to toxic materials, safeguarding the well-being of crew members and protecting coastal communities from potential environmental disasters.

Moreover, responsible practices in pollution prevention and control directly contribute to health and safety. By adhering to best practices in ballast water management, waste disposal, and emissions reduction, the maritime industry mitigates the release of harmful substances into the environment. This not only benefits marine ecosystems but also limits health risks to maritime personnel who would otherwise be exposed to pollutants. In essence, the industry's commitment to environmental responsibility aligns with its commitment to worker safety, creating a safer and more sustainable maritime workplace.

The maritime industry's pursuit of improved environmental practices is intrinsically linked to enhancing health and safety. Stringent safety protocols, reduced exposure to hazardous substances, and minimised pollution risks are all integral to responsible practices. These measures collectively contribute to the well-being of maritime personnel and the safety of communities near maritime operations. Ultimately, a commitment to environmental and occupational safety is a testament to the industry's dedication to creating a secure and sustainable future.

1. **INNOVATION AND COMPETITIVENESS**

Embracing sustainability within the maritime industry catalyses innovation. As companies prioritise environmentally responsible practices, they often channel resources into research and development efforts to create cleaner technologies and alternative propulsion systems. These innovations not only contribute to environmental stewardship but also enhance competitiveness within the industry. Companies at the vanguard of these advancements position themselves as industry leaders, uniquely equipped to meet evolving market demands and regulatory requirements.

Innovation in sustainability extends across various aspects of maritime operations. From developing energy-efficient vessel designs to integrating renewable energy sources and implementing advanced emission reduction technologies, forward-thinking companies continually seek novel solutions. Such innovation aligns with global sustainability goals and affords companies a competitive edge. It allows them to meet customer demands for environmentally friendly services easily, navigate evolving regulatory landscapes, and reduce operational costs through energy-efficient practices.

The embrace of sustainability within the maritime industry fosters innovation that extends well beyond environmental benefits. These innovations contribute to a company's competitive advantages by enabling it to stay ahead of industry trends, regulatory changes, and customer preferences. By positioning themselves as pioneers in sustainable maritime practices, companies enhance their market competitiveness and solidify their standing as industry leaders.

1. **COMMUNITY ENGAGEMENT**

Embracing responsible practices within the maritime industry goes beyond environmental considerations; it also plays a pivotal role in fostering positive relationships with coastal communities and stakeholders. Through active engagement with local communities, addressing environmental concerns, and contributing to sustainable development initiatives, maritime companies can cultivate a social license to operate and garner essential support for their activities.

One of the fundamental aspects of community engagement is the proactive communication of environmental efforts. By openly sharing information about sustainability initiatives and the steps taken to minimise environmental impact, maritime companies demonstrate transparency and accountability. This communication raises awareness and invites feedback from local communities, allowing them to express their concerns and opinions. In response, companies can adapt their practices to align better with community expectations, creating a more harmonious relationship.

Furthermore, responsible practices often extend to community involvement and support. Maritime companies frequently engage in initiatives that contribute to the well-being of coastal communities, such as sponsoring local environmental projects, participating in community clean-up events, or providing job opportunities. These contributions demonstrate corporate social responsibility and help build trust and goodwill. As coastal communities recognise the positive impact of responsible maritime operations on their environment and quality of life, they are more likely to lend their support, further strengthening the social foundation upon which the industry operates.

Community engagement is a crucial facet of responsible maritime practices. By actively involving coastal communities, addressing their environmental concerns, and contributing to their sustainable development, maritime companies can secure a social license to operate. This social support is invaluable for the industry, as it helps build bridges between stakeholders, mitigates potential conflicts, and reinforces the industry's commitment to environmental stewardship and the well-being of the communities it serves.

1. RISK MITIGATION

Adopting sustainable practices within the maritime industry plays a pivotal role in mitigating a spectrum of risks associated with climate change. Climate-related challenges, including rising sea levels and increasingly frequent extreme weather events, threaten maritime operations and coastal communities. Implementing proactive measures to reduce emissions and adapt to changing environmental conditions enhances the industry's operational resilience and safeguards against these multifaceted risks.

One of the primary risks sustainable practices help mitigate is the impact of rising sea levels. As climate change leads to higher sea levels, coastal regions become more susceptible to flooding and erosion. Maritime infrastructure, such as ports and terminals, can be severely affected. By prioritising sustainability, maritime companies take steps to reduce greenhouse gas emissions, contributing to global efforts to curb sea-level rise. Additionally, sustainable ship designs often consider future sea-level scenarios, ensuring vessels can navigate in altered conditions and minimise the risk of accidents or damage to maritime assets.

Extreme weather events, another climate change-related risk, have the potential to disrupt maritime operations significantly. Sustainable practices encourage resilience planning and disaster preparedness. Companies embracing sustainability often invest in advanced forecasting and monitoring systems, allowing them to anticipate and respond to weather-related risks proactively. Furthermore, they may implement safety protocols, such as diversifying routes to avoid storm-prone areas or enhancing vessel designs to withstand severe weather conditions. These proactive measures enhance the industry's capacity to operate safely and reliably in the face of climate-induced challenges.

Sustainable practices are pivotal in mitigating climate change-related risks for the maritime industry. By reducing emissions, adapting to changing environmental conditions, and prioritising operational resilience, maritime companies can safeguard their operations and contribute to the broader effort to address climate challenges. These proactive measures protect maritime assets and enhance the industry's long-term viability and sustainability in a changing climate landscape.

1. GLOBAL SUSTAINABILITY GOALS

The maritime industry is crucial in achieving global sustainability goals, such as those outlined in the United Nations' Sustainable Development Goals (SDGs). Environmentally responsible practices align with these goals, contributing to broader efforts to combat climate change and protect the oceans.

Environmentally responsible practices in the maritime sector offer multifaceted benefits. They promote economic resilience, reduce environmental harm, enhance safety, and position the industry as a key player in achieving global sustainability objectives. By embracing responsible practices, the maritime sector safeguards its future and contributes to a more sustainable and resilient planet.

Chapter 18

GREEN SHIPPING IN A CHANGING CLIMATE

The maritime industry operates at the intersection of environmental and climate challenges, making it imperative to address the impacts of climate change while pursuing sustainable shipping practices. Chapter 18 delves into the multifaceted relationship between green shipping and a changing climate, offering insights into how the industry navigates this complex terrain.

THE IMPACT OF CLIMATE CHANGE ON MARITIME SHIPPING

The impact of climate change on maritime shipping is a multifaceted challenge encompassing various dimensions, from operational risks to environmental consequences. Here, we explore these impacts in detail:

- **Rising Sea Levels:** One of the most visible consequences of climate change is the rise in global sea levels. This phenomenon directly affects maritime infrastructure, including ports, terminals, and coastal facilities. As sea levels increase, ports and harbours face the threat of inundation and erosion. This can disrupt shipping operations, damage infrastructure, and lead to costly repairs and adaptations.
- **Extreme Weather Events:** Climate change contributes to the intensification and frequency of extreme weather events, such as hurricanes, cyclones, and typhoons. These events pose significant risks to vessels at sea and port facilities. Shipping routes can be disrupted, and vessels may need to change course or seek shelter, leading to delays and increased operational costs.
- **Changing Ocean Conditions:** Altered oceanic conditions, including changes in temperature and salinity, impact marine ecosystems and shipping operations. Rising sea surface temperatures can affect vessel engine efficiency and increase the risk of engine overheating. Additionally, changes in ocean currents may require shipping routes and navigation adjustments.
- **Increased Storm Intensity:** Climate change contributes to the intensification of storms, leading to rougher seas and higher waves. This poses safety concerns for vessels and crew members. Severe storms can damage ships, cargo, and onboard equipment, resulting in financial losses and safety risks.
- **Ice Melt in Polar Regions:** The melting of polar ice caps due to rising temperatures opens up new shipping routes in previously inaccessible areas, such as the Arctic. While this offers shorter transit times and cost savings opportunities, it also raises environmental concerns. Increased shipping activity in these fragile ecosystems can

lead to oil spills, habitat disruption, and a heightened risk of accidents in ice-infested waters.
- **Operational Challenges:** Climate change can lead to operational challenges for vessels. Higher sea temperatures can affect the cooling systems of engines, potentially leading to reduced efficiency and increased maintenance costs. Additionally, extreme weather events and changing weather patterns require careful navigation and route planning to ensure the safety of crew, cargo, and vessels.
- **Environmental Impact:** Climate change has far-reaching environmental consequences, and the maritime industry is not immune. Ocean acidification, caused by the absorption of excess carbon dioxide by the oceans, can harm marine life and ecosystems. Shipping activities, including ballast water discharge and oil spills, can exacerbate these environmental challenges.
- **Regulatory Response:** To address climate change, governments and international organisations implement regulations and emissions reduction targets. This directly impacts the maritime industry, which is under pressure to reduce greenhouse gas emissions. Compliance with these regulations may require investments in cleaner technologies, alternative fuels, and emissions reduction strategies.
- **Supply Chain Disruptions:** Climate-related disruptions can affect the entire supply chain, impacting cargo handling, storage, and distribution. Ports and terminals may experience delays and congestion due to extreme weather events or rising sea levels, affecting the flow of goods and increasing logistics costs.
- **Financial Risks:** Climate-related risks, including damage to vessels, cargo, and infrastructure, can result in financial losses for maritime companies. Increased insurance premiums and liability for environmental damage are among the financial challenges associated with climate change impacts.

The impact of climate change on maritime shipping encompasses a wide range of challenges that affect vessel operations, safety, infrastructure, and the environment. Navigating these challenges requires proactive measures, including investments in resilience, emissions reduction, and compliance with evolving regulations, to ensure the long-term sustainability and adaptability of the maritime industry in a changing climate.

ADAPTATION AND RESILIENCE STRATEGIES FOR GREEN SHIPPING

Adaptation and resilience strategies for green shipping are essential to mitigate the impacts of climate change and ensure the industry's long-term sustainability. These strategies encompass a wide range of measures, both operational and technological.

Here's a comprehensive overview of these strategies:

1. **IMPROVED WEATHER FORECASTING AND ROUTE PLANNING**

Utilising advanced weather forecasting technologies, shipping companies can receive real-time weather updates and plan routes to avoid extreme weather conditions. This minimises the risks associated with storms and reduces the likelihood of accidents or vessel damage.

2. **VESSEL DESIGN AND RETROFITTING**

Investing in vessel designs that enhance stability and weather resistance is crucial. Innovations like wave-piercing hulls and advanced stabilisers can help ships navigate rough seas more effectively. Retrofitting existing vessels with these technologies can also improve their resilience.

3. **ALTERNATIVE FUELS AND PROPULSION SYSTEMS**

Transitioning to alternative fuels, such as liquefied natural gas (LNG), hydrogen, or ammonia, reduces the carbon footprint of shipping operations. These fuels emit fewer greenhouse gases and are less sensitive to adverse weather conditions. Additionally, exploring renewable propulsion systems, such as wind-assist technologies or sail-assisted propulsion, can enhance vessel resilience.

4. **FUEL EFFICIENCY AND ENERGY MANAGEMENT**

Implementing fuel-efficient technologies and energy management systems onboard vessels can reduce fuel consumption and improve operational efficiency. Measures include optimising engine performance, reducing idling time, and investing in hybrid or electric propulsion systems.

5. **EMERGENCY RESPONSE PROTOCOLS**

Developing comprehensive emergency response protocols and training crew members to react to extreme weather events is essential. This includes procedures for securing cargo, battening down hatches, and ensuring the safety of the crew during adverse conditions.

6. **INVESTMENT IN GREEN PORTS**

Ports and terminals play a critical role in maritime operations. Investing in green port infrastructure, such as resilient berths, stormwater management systems, and sustainable energy sources, enhances a port's ability to withstand climate-related disruptions.

7. **DIGITAL TECHNOLOGIES**

Leveraging digital technologies like Internet of Things (IoT) sensors and data analytics can provide real-time insights into vessel performance and weather conditions. This data can help operators make informed decisions and adjust routes or operations to improve resilience.

1. **DIVERSIFICATION OF SHIPPING ROUTES**

Relying on a single shipping route can be risky due to changing weather patterns. Diversifying shipping routes and avoiding areas prone to extreme weather events can reduce exposure to climate-related risks.

1. **COLLABORATION AND INFORMATION SHARING**

Collaboration among shipping companies, ports, and maritime authorities is essential for disaster preparedness and response. Sharing information about weather conditions, navigational hazards, and emergency resources can improve the industry's collective resilience.

1. **CLIMATE RISK ASSESSMENT**

Conducting thorough climate risk assessments helps shipping companies identify vulnerabilities and develop tailored resilience strategies. These assessments should consider long-term climate projections and the specific risks associated with the regions in which vessels operate.

1. **INSURANCE AND RISK MANAGEMENT**

Ensuring vessels have adequate insurance coverage for climate-related risks is essential. This includes coverage for damage caused by extreme weather events and pollution liability insurance in case of accidents.

1. **INVESTMENT IN RESEARCH AND DEVELOPMENT**

Continued investment in research and development is crucial for the maritime industry to stay at the forefront of green and resilient technologies. This includes research into alternative fuels, vessel designs, and climate-resilient infrastructure.

By adopting these adaptation and resilience strategies, the maritime industry can better prepare for the challenges posed by climate change while advancing its commitment to green shipping practices. These measures not only enhance the industry's ability to withstand climate-related disruptions but also contribute to reducing its environmental impact.

THE ROLE OF SHIPPING IN MITIGATING CLIMATE CHANGE

The role of shipping in mitigating climate change is paramount, given its substantial contribution to global greenhouse gas (GHG) emissions and its potential to adopt environmentally responsible practices. Shipping operations are responsible for a significant share of emissions, primarily from the combustion of fossil fuels like heavy oil and diesel. Consequently, the industry carries a dual responsibility and opportunity to address climate change by reducing emissions and pioneering sustainable solutions.

One of the most immediate actions the maritime sector can take to mitigate climate change is transitioning to cleaner fuels and propulsion systems. Liquefied natural gas (LNG), hydrogen, ammonia, and biofuels are emerging as promising alternatives to traditional marine fuels.

When burned, these alternatives produce fewer GHG emissions, and their adoption can significantly curtail the sector's carbon footprint.

Energy efficiency is another key focus area for climate change mitigation in shipping. Embracing advanced technologies and operational practices can substantially reduce emissions during voyages. This includes optimising vessel designs for improved hydrodynamics, investing in energy-efficient engines and hull coatings, and adopting smart navigation systems that optimise routes for fuel savings.

Additionally, slow steaming—operating vessels at lower speeds—can lead to substantial fuel savings and emissions reductions. When combined with other efficiency measures, this strategy contributes to a greener and more sustainable industry.

Innovative vessel designs are critical in the maritime industry's efforts to mitigate climate change. Concepts like wind-assist or sail-assisted propulsion systems harness renewable energy sources to augment propulsion, further enhancing fuel efficiency and lowering emissions. These innovations are part of a broader shift towards more sustainable ship designs.

However, the maritime sector must act in collaboration to address climate change. Collaborative endeavours among industry stakeholders, regulatory bodies, and the global community are essential. International agreements, such as the International Maritime Organisation's (IMO) greenhouse gas reduction targets, set a framework for emissions reduction efforts. Cooperative initiatives, knowledge sharing, and technological advancements are pivotal in achieving these goals.

In conclusion, the maritime industry occupies a critical position in the fight against climate change. Its commitment to adopting cleaner fuels, improving energy efficiency, and exploring innovative vessel designs is central to the global effort to reduce GHG emissions and mitigate the impacts of climate change. By embracing sustainability and green shipping practices, the sector can reduce its environmental footprint and serve as a beacon of innovation and responsibility in addressing one of the world's most pressing challenges.

Chapter 19

PUBLIC PERCEPTION AND CONSUMER DEMAND

Public perception and consumer demand are pivotal in transforming the maritime industry to green and sustainable practices. This chapter delves into the intricate relationship between public opinion, consumer preferences, and the maritime sector's response to meet evolving expectations.

The maritime industry operates in an increasingly interconnected world where information flows freely. Media coverage and public awareness campaigns highlighting environmental issues, such as marine pollution and climate change, have sensitised communities and consumers to the ecological impact of maritime activities. This heightened awareness has led to greater scrutiny of industry practices and, in turn, a demand for more sustainable and responsible operations. Consumers are becoming more discerning, seeking goods and services provided by companies that align with their values. As a result, maritime companies that embrace sustainable practices meet regulatory requirements and tap into a growing market of environmentally conscious consumers who prioritise products and services with a lower environmental footprint.

Furthermore, public perception significantly influences regulatory frameworks and government policies. Elected officials often respond to the concerns of their constituents, and as public awareness of environmental issues grows, governments are increasingly inclined to enact stricter regulations. The maritime industry's response to public sentiment and consumer demand can proactively shape regulatory developments. By demonstrating a commitment to sustainability, companies can influence the trajectory of regulations, ensuring that they are practical and conducive to industry growth while also addressing environmental concerns. In this way, public perception and consumer demand serve as catalysts for positive change within the maritime sector, fostering a mutually beneficial relationship between industry, society, and the environment.

PUBLIC AWARENESS AND DEMAND FOR SUSTAINABLE SHIPPING

Public awareness and demand for sustainable shipping have experienced a remarkable surge in recent years, propelled by an unprecedented surge in environmental consciousness and a deep-seated desire among consumers to make ethically responsible choices. This discernible shift in public perception holds profound and far-reaching implications for the maritime industry, exerting substantial influence on its operational practices, strategic priorities, and overall responsiveness to mounting environmental and social concerns.

An increasing recognition of the interconnectedness of the global ecosystem and the detrimental effects of climate change has driven the remarkable transformation in public sentiment towards sustainability. Citizens across the globe have become more acutely aware of the fragility of marine ecosystems and the profound impacts of maritime activities on the planet's health. This growing awareness has galvanised a broad-based movement demanding eco-friendly, ethical, and responsible practices from the maritime sector. Now armed with a heightened sense of environmental responsibility, consumers are scrutinising maritime companies' practices and seeking products and services that align with their values.

The resonance of this collective environmental consciousness has had a ripple effect across the maritime industry. It has necessitated a profound re-evaluation of operational standards, exploring innovative green technologies, and accelerating the adoption of sustainable practices. Maritime companies, in response to this burgeoning demand, are transitioning towards more eco-conscious approaches, underlining their commitment to environmental stewardship. This shift signifies an acknowledgement of evolving consumer preferences and a recognition of the industry's responsibility to operate in harmony with the environment. Consequently, the maritime industry finds itself at a critical juncture, where the convergence of public awareness and demand compels it to chart a course towards a greener, more sustainable future.

EVOLVING PUBLIC AWARENESS

Public consciousness regarding the environmental impact of shipping has undergone a significant expansion in recent years. This amplification in awareness stems from the greater accessibility of information relating to pollution, emissions, and the profound ecological ramifications of maritime activities. Environmental organisations, the pervasive reach of media coverage, and educational campaigns have played a pivotal and instrumental role in catalysing this transformation.

As the digital age has ushered in an era of unprecedented information sharing and connectivity, individuals worldwide have gained unparalleled access to data and insights regarding the environmental toll of maritime operations. Environmental organisations and advocacy groups have leveraged digital platforms to disseminate compelling narratives, impactful statistics, and real-life accounts of ecological harm wrought by certain shipping practices. This information dissemination has cultivated a heightened sense of responsibility and urgency among the general public, spurring them to engage more actively with marine conservation and environmental sustainability issues.

Moreover, the power of the media cannot be overstated in this context. Extensive media coverage in traditional and digital formats has brought environmental concerns to the forefront of public discourse. Documentary films, investigative journalism, and compelling stories have vividly portrayed the challenges marine ecosystems and coastal communities face due to irresponsible maritime activities. As these narratives have reached a global audience, they have triggered a collective awakening to the environmental consequences of shipping, propelling environmental considerations to the forefront of public consciousness.

Simultaneously, educational campaigns have emerged as essential for fostering this expanding awareness. Educational initiatives, from school curricula to community workshops, have worked diligently to equip individuals with the knowledge and tools to comprehend and address maritime environmental issues. These campaigns have empowered citizens to make informed decisions and advocate for sustainable practices, creating a ripple effect that resonates throughout society.

In essence, the evolving public awareness of the environmental impact of shipping represents a profound shift in societal attitudes towards responsible and sustainable maritime practices. This transformation, catalysed by the convergence of information, media influence, and educational endeavours, stands as a testament to the potency of collective action in promoting environmental stewardship within the maritime sector.

ENVIRONMENTAL CONCERNS

The escalating preoccupation of the public with pressing global issues such as climate change, pollution, and the degradation of delicate ecosystems has triggered a substantial surge in interest in sustainable shipping practices. This burgeoning awareness indicates a populace becoming progressively attuned to the urgency of mitigating these environmental challenges. Individuals worldwide are increasingly conscious of the imperatives to curtail greenhouse gas emissions, safeguard the integrity of marine ecosystems, and actively mitigate the expansive carbon footprint entailed by the vast realm of global trade.

The profound shift in societal sentiment can be attributed to several converging factors. Foremost among these is the mounting body of scientific evidence affirming the human role in accelerating climate change and its far-reaching consequences. This scientific consensus, supported by comprehensive research and data, has underscored the criticality of immediate action to curb emissions and mitigate the detrimental impacts of climate change. As the public increasingly absorbs this knowledge, they are compelled to scrutinise the ecological impact of industries like shipping that play a pivotal role in the global economy.

Furthermore, the ecological devastation wrought by pollution, particularly in marine environments, has garnered widespread attention. Distressing images of plastic-choked oceans, oil spills, and biodiversity loss have imprinted on the collective conscience. These visual reminders of the fragility of our natural world have catalysed a sense of responsibility among individuals, pushing them to demand cleaner, more sustainable shipping practices.

Additionally, the interconnectedness of our globalised world has heightened awareness of the vast carbon footprint of international trade and shipping. As consumers, citizens, and environmental advocates become increasingly cognizant of the emissions generated by transporting goods across continents, they call for greater transparency, accountability, and eco-friendly alternatives within the shipping industry.

The heightened public concern about climate change, pollution, and the deterioration of ecosystems is a testament to the growing recognition of the pivotal role that sustainable shipping plays in addressing these global challenges. This transformative shift in public sentiment emphasises the imperative for the maritime sector to adopt greener, more responsible practices that align with the aspirations of a world increasingly committed to environmental stewardship.

CONSUMER PREFERENCES

A notable transformation is underway in the realm of consumer preferences, marked by a discernible shift towards products and services that resonate with their deeply held sustainability values. Central to this evolving consumer mindset is a burgeoning inclination for goods that are not just high in quality but also reach them through the conduit of environmentally responsible shipping companies.

Whether driven by an eco-conscious conscience or a desire to effect meaningful change, the contemporary consumer is showing a marked proclivity to patronise businesses that have elevated sustainability to a central tenet of their supply chains and logistics.

This perceptible shift in consumer behaviour indicates a profound attitudinal shift towards responsible consumption. Today's consumers, armed with easy access to information and growing ecological awareness, are increasingly prepared to make choices that reflect their values. Beyond merely seeking products, they are deliberately supporting businesses that share their commitment to sustainability.

This manifests as a preference for companies that provide high-quality offerings and champion ethical, eco-friendly practices throughout their operations. The evolving consumer drives businesses to reevaluate their supply chain strategies, adopt cleaner transportation methods, and embrace sustainability as a cornerstone of their brand identity.

This transition is not merely a trend but a fundamental transformation in how products and services are sought, valued, and consumed in today's conscientious marketplace.

TRANSPARENCY AND ACCOUNTABILITY

In the contemporary business landscape, transparency in corporate practices has graduated from a desirable attribute to an absolute core expectation. This profound shift is prominently visible in responsible shipping, where consumers now insist upon unambiguous and comprehensive information regarding a company's environmental endeavours, emissions reduction strategies, and unequivocal commitment to responsible logistics. Today's discerning consumers, motivated by a genuine desire to enact positive change and make choices that resonate with their values, have propelled transparency to the forefront of their purchasing considerations.

This growing demand for transparency and accountability represents a discernible shift in consumer sentiment. In an era of unprecedented access to information, individuals are no longer content with superficial corporate claims of eco-friendliness. Instead, they seek concrete evidence of a company's environmental dedication, ranging from emissions reduction targets and sustainable sourcing practices to adherence to stringent environmental regulations. This push for transparency underscores an essential realisation among consumers that informed choices are not just an exercise in personal responsibility but a powerful lever for influencing positive change in the business world. As such, it places a paramount onus on companies to implement sustainable practices and communicate them transparently, empowering consumers to make decisions that align with their values and the greater good.

CERTIFICATIONS AND ECO-LABELS

In the evolving landscape of sustainable shipping, certifications and eco-labels have emerged as pivotal tools that bridge the gap between consumer demand for eco-conscious products and the maritime industry's commitment to responsible practices.

These certifications, exemplified by the Clean Shipping Index and the Green Marine certification program, hold profound significance in meeting and surpassing the expectations of today's environmentally aware consumers.

They serve as tangible assurances that shipping companies are not merely making claims but actively adhering to stringent environmental standards, thus facilitating and simplifying the process of making eco-conscious consumer choices.

These certifications and eco-labels embody accountability and commitment within the maritime sector. They are emblematic of the industry's recognition that transparency and responsible practices are non-negotiable. In the eyes of consumers, these labels signify a dedication to ecological stewardship and sustainability beyond mere words.

They serve as valuable indicators that a shipping company has subjected itself to rigorous scrutiny, aligning its operations with environmentally sound principles. As a result, consumers are provided with the confidence that their choices bear a direct positive impact on the environment. Certifications and eco-labels thus serve as powerful tools for translating a shipping company's sustainability initiatives into comprehensible symbols of trust, facilitating informed decisions among consumers seeking to champion responsible shipping practices.

INFLUENCE OF SOCIAL MEDIA

The pervasive influence of social media in the digital age cannot be overstated, particularly regarding issues of environmental advocacy and sustainability within the maritime industry. These platforms have metamorphosed into potent tools that empower environmental activists and concerned citizens to amplify their voices, galvanise movements, and effectively shape public discourse. This collective voice, resonating through social media channels, has the power to exert significant pressure on shipping companies, compelling them to adopt greener practices and respond proactively to the public's environmental concerns.

One of the defining features of social media is its capacity to democratise communication. Environmental activists and concerned citizens, irrespective of their geographical location or social standing, can harness the reach of social platforms to draw attention to issues like carbon emissions, ocean pollution, and responsible shipping practices. The viral nature of social media campaigns can quickly transform localised concerns into global conversations, placing shipping companies under a spotlight where they must reckon with the expectations of an increasingly eco-conscious public.

Moreover, social media serves as an indispensable tool for transparency and accountability. Environmental activists and consumers quickly scrutinise and share information about a company's environmental performance, from emissions data to sustainability initiatives. In the era of instant information dissemination, shipping companies are acutely aware that their positive and negative actions can be amplified exponentially through these platforms. This awareness, in turn, incentivises proactive responses as companies seek to align their practices with the values and expectations of a socially connected world.

Social media platforms have engendered a paradigm shift in the landscape of environmental advocacy, enabling citizens and activists to leverage their collective influence to foster change within the maritime industry. The rapid dissemination of information, the capacity to mobilise public sentiment, and the power to hold companies accountable all underscore social media's undeniable influence in catalysing the transition towards greener, more responsible shipping practices.

MARKET COMPETITIVENESS

The contemporary maritime industry finds itself at the nexus of economic viability and environmental stewardship, where the pursuit of sustainability has become an ethical and strategic imperative. This pivotal shift is underscored by the recognition among shipping companies that embracing greener technologies and practices is not just about altruism but also about securing a prominent foothold in a market where consumers progressively gravitate towards environmentally responsible choices. In essence, market competitiveness has transformed, with sustainability now a linchpin of success.

Companies within the maritime sector are acutely aware that the economic advantages of sustainability are multifaceted. Reduced fuel consumption through improved energy efficiency directly translates into cost savings, bolstering their financial bottom line. Moreover, investments in green technologies, such as cleaner propulsion systems and alternative fuels, position these companies for long-term economic benefits by mitigating the impact of volatile fossil fuel prices and regulatory changes. As such, market competitiveness in today's shipping industry is not merely predicated on traditional metrics. However, it is intrinsically tied to a company's capacity to align with the growing demand for sustainability, thereby securing its relevance and profitability in an evolving marketplace.

POLICY AND REGULATION

In the ever-evolving landscape of the maritime industry, the realm of policy and regulation stands as a pivotal catalyst in propelling the sector towards greater environmental responsibility. Government regulations, shaped by a tapestry of factors including public opinion and environmental consciousness, are transforming profoundly. These evolving regulations are charting a course towards setting stricter emissions standards and heightened environmental requirements for maritime operations, thus setting the regulatory framework for greener practices within the industry.

The symbiotic relationship between public pressure and regulatory change cannot be overstated. Public opinion, often channelled and amplified through avenues like social media and environmental activism, holds the potential to instigate seismic shifts in government policy. As the public becomes increasingly conscious of the environmental consequences of maritime activities, it exercises its influence to advocate for more stringent regulations that compel shipping companies to adopt greener practices. Consequently, the maritime industry is confronted with a twofold impetus: to align with the prevailing and forthcoming regulations to maintain compliance and proactively embrace greener technologies and practices to ensure adherence and secure a competitive edge in a market where sustainability is progressively non-negotiable. The nexus of policy and regulation represents a linchpin in catalysing the industry's transition towards a more environmentally conscious future.

COMMUNITY ENGAGEMENT

In today's maritime landscape, community engagement has emerged as a strategic imperative that shipping companies increasingly recognise and prioritise. These companies acknowledge the profound importance of forging meaningful connections with local communities directly impacted by their operations. In doing so, they are not only fostering goodwill but also actively addressing the concerns and needs of these communities. Such endeavours contribute to a positive public perception and engender vital community support.

The significance of community engagement within the maritime sector extends far beyond mere tokenism. It reflects a genuine commitment to social responsibility and sustainability, where shipping companies recognise that their operations can significantly impact the lives, livelihoods, and environments of the communities they serve. Meaningful interactions with these communities entail listening to their concerns, collaborating on solutions, and establishing channels for ongoing dialogue. By doing so, shipping companies demonstrate their commitment to responsible practices and build trust and credibility, which are foundational to securing social license and fostering harmonious relationships with their communities. Ultimately, community engagement reflects an industry's broader evolution towards greater environmental and social consciousness, where the well-being of communities becomes intrinsically tied to its success and sustainability.

ENVIRONMENTAL EDUCATION

In the modern maritime industry, the role of environmental education has blossomed into a pivotal force shaping both public awareness and individual responsibility. Initiatives and outreach programs geared towards promoting sustainable shipping and marine conservation are instrumental, serving as potent vehicles for enhancing public knowledge and instilling a profound sense of environmental responsibility.

These educational endeavours transcend mere information dissemination; they are transformative experiences that empower individuals with a deeper understanding of the complex interplay between maritime activities and environmental health. Such programs often illuminate the ecological consequences of shipping, ranging from carbon emissions and pollution to the conservation of marine ecosystems. They engage the public in an active dialogue about the maritime industry's environmental impact and the collective responsibility to mitigate it.

Consequently, environmental education acts as a catalyst, fostering a culture of stewardship and sustainability, where individuals, communities, and even the industry are inspired to take meaningful actions supporting responsible maritime practices. In this evolving landscape, environmental education is an indispensable thread in the maritime industry's journey towards greater environmental consciousness and accountability.

Public awareness and demand for sustainable shipping are driving forces behind the maritime industry's transition to greener and more responsible practices. As consumers increasingly prioritise sustainability in their choices, shipping companies must adapt, innovate, and align their operations with the growing expectations for environmentally responsible shipping. This shift towards sustainability benefits the environment and positions the maritime sector as a key player in addressing global environmental challenges.

MARKETING AND BRANDING STRATEGIES FOR GREEN SHIPPING COMPANIES

Marketing and branding strategies for green shipping companies are vital to effectively communicate their commitment to sustainability, differentiate themselves in the market, and attract environmentally conscious customers. Here are key strategies to consider:

1. CLEAR SUSTAINABILITY MESSAGING

One of the foundational elements in steering a maritime company towards a more sustainable future is the development of a clear and compelling sustainability messaging strategy. This involves crafting a narrative that underscores the company's unwavering commitment to eco-friendly practices and emphasises the positive impact of these initiatives on the environment. The efficacy of this messaging lies in its ability to resonate with various stakeholders, from customers to investors, and inspire confidence in the company's dedication to sustainability.

To achieve this, the use of clear and concise language is pivotal. Complex technical jargon or explanations can obscure the company's green initiatives and associated benefits. Instead, the messaging should be easily digestible and accessible to a broad audience. It should transparently convey the company's efforts to reduce its environmental footprint through emission reductions, energy-efficient technologies, or sustainable sourcing practices.

By encapsulating these elements within a succinct and compelling sustainability narrative, maritime companies can communicate their commitment to eco-friendly practices and foster greater trust and engagement with stakeholders who increasingly prioritise sustainability in their decision-making processes.

2. SUSTAINABLE BRAND IDENTITY

In pursuing a more sustainable maritime future, crafting a sustainable brand identity emerges as a potent strategy. This approach entails integrating eco-friendly elements into a company's brand identity, effectively imbuing its visual and verbal representations with a commitment to environmental responsibility. This can manifest in various ways, such as adopting green colour schemes, incorporating logos featuring eco-symbols, or employing taglines that prominently emphasise sustainability.

The symbiosis between sustainable branding and a company's core values is crucial. For a brand to authentically communicate its dedication to green shipping, it must do more than adorn itself with environmentally conscious aesthetics. The branding should genuinely reflect the company's ethos, practices, and overarching mission. When these elements align harmoniously, a sustainable brand identity can become a powerful tool, fostering brand recognition and loyalty among customers who value eco-friendly businesses. It also serves as a tangible testament to the company's commitment to sustainability. It establishes a profound connection with stakeholders and positions the maritime company as a leading advocate for green practices within the industry.

3. CERTIFICATION AND ECO-LABELS

In the quest for a sustainable maritime identity, the acquisition and prominent display of relevant sustainability certifications and eco-labels take centre stage. These credentials, such as the Clean Shipping Index or ISO 14001, are invaluable third-party validations of a company's eco-friendly practices. They substantiate the company's commitment to environmental responsibility and lend credibility to its sustainability claims.

However, the efficacy of these certifications extends beyond the mere acquisition; it hinges on educating customers about their significance. Through clear and transparent communication, maritime companies can convey the importance of these certifications, elucidating how they mirror the company's dedication to sustainable practices. By empowering customers with an understanding of these certifications, companies foster trust and confidence. Customers are assured that they are supporting a business that adheres to rigorous environmental standards, incentivising sustainable choices and furthering the maritime industry's journey towards a greener future.

4. EDUCATIONAL CONTENT

A pivotal strategy in steering maritime companies toward sustainability involves the creation of informative content that serves as a beacon of knowledge for customers. This educational content can take various forms, including blogs, articles, webinars, and more, and its primary objective is to enlighten customers about sustainable shipping practices, emissions reduction strategies, and environmental protection.

By disseminating valuable insights and knowledge, maritime companies can position themselves as industry leaders, pioneering change and setting new standards in the industry. This role as an educator enhances the company's reputation and instils confidence in customers, who seek reliable and informed partners in their pursuit of sustainability. Furthermore, this educational content can catalyse change beyond the company itself, as it empowers customers to make informed decisions that align with eco-friendly values. By championing knowledge sharing and actively contributing to the environmental discourse, maritime companies can play an instrumental role in fostering a more sustainable and conscientious industry.

5. GREEN PARTNERSHIPS

An instrumental stride toward maritime sustainability involves forging collaborative alliances with other eco-conscious organisations, non-governmental organisations (NGOs), or environmental initiatives. These partnerships are the bedrock of collective action, amplifying a company's commitment to sustainability.

When showcased in marketing materials, these collaborations serve as visible testaments to the company's dedication to making a positive impact. Highlighting these partnerships underscores the company's role as a proactive and responsible player in the quest for a greener maritime industry. Moreover, these partnerships contribute to sharing knowledge, resources, and innovative solutions, fostering a more robust and interconnected network of sustainability advocates within the industry. By joining forces with like-minded entities, maritime companies can synergise their efforts, accelerate change, and collectively work toward a future where sustainable shipping practices are the norm rather than the exception.

6. SHOWCASE ECO-FRIENDLY TECHNOLOGIES

A powerful strategy for maritime companies on the sustainability journey is to prominently display the innovative technologies and eco-friendly practices they have adopted. This can encompass a wide range of initiatives, from utilising alternative fuels and energy-efficient vessels to implementing emissions reduction measures.

One effective means of showcasing these efforts is through case studies or videos. These materials provide concrete, real-world examples of how these technologies contribute to a greener shipping industry. They offer transparency and insight into the practical implementation of sustainability measures and can be a compelling way to communicate the company's commitment to environmentally responsible practices. By sharing success stories and tangible results, maritime companies can inspire others to embrace similar technologies and contribute to a collective transformation toward a more sustainable and eco-conscious future.

7. SOCIAL MEDIA ENGAGEMENT:

In the age of digital connectivity, maintaining an active and dynamic presence on social media platforms is paramount for maritime companies committed to sustainability. These platforms are vital communication channels through which companies can interact with customers and stakeholders and share updates on their ongoing sustainability efforts.

One effective strategy is to encourage user-generated content related to green initiatives. This approach invites customers to participate in the company's sustainability journey actively, creating a sense of community and shared responsibility. By sharing and amplifying user-generated content, maritime companies demonstrate their commitment to sustainability and foster a deeper and more authentic connection with their audience. Furthermore, social media provides a real-time avenue for dialogue and feedback, enabling companies to gauge public sentiment, address concerns, and refine their sustainability strategies. In essence, social media engagement can serve as a dynamic and interactive platform for propagating sustainability principles and forging a strong bond between the maritime industry and its eco-conscious community.

8. CUSTOMER TESTIMONIALS

Harnessing the power of customer testimonials can be a compelling approach for maritime companies dedicated to sustainable practices. These testimonials serve as authentic endorsements of a company's green shipping services and can significantly influence the opinions and decisions of potential customers.

By featuring customer testimonials or success stories that highlight positive experiences with eco-friendly shipping services, maritime companies can build trust and credibility within their customer base. These firsthand accounts offer insights into the tangible benefits of choosing sustainable shipping options, such as reduced environmental impact and reliable service. Moreover, customer testimonials humanise the sustainability narrative, making it relatable and accessible to a broader audience. They showcase the real-world impact of eco-conscious choices and reinforce that sustainability is not just a corporate commitment but a practical and rewarding choice for customers. In essence, these testimonials become persuasive narratives that underscore a company's dedication to delivering value and sustainability hand in hand.

9. SUSTAINABILITY REPORTS

Annual sustainability reports are a cornerstone of transparent communication for maritime companies striving to be eco-conscious. These reports serve as comprehensive documents detailing a company's environmental achievements, emissions reductions, and progress toward sustainability goals.

To maximise their impact, these reports should be made readily accessible to the public and stakeholders. By sharing these reports openly, companies demonstrate a commitment to transparency and accountability. They offer a detailed account of the company's sustainability journey, outlining successes and challenges. Moreover, these reports provide a platform for showcasing tangible results and the positive environmental impact of the company's efforts.

In essence, sustainability reports serve as a window into the company's sustainability performance, fostering trust and enabling stakeholders to track progress and hold the company accountable for its commitments. They reinforce the notion that sustainability is not just a slogan but a quantifiable and ongoing endeavour firmly embedded in the company's operational DNA.

10. GREEN PACKAGING AND MATERIALS:

Embracing eco-friendly packaging and materials is pivotal for maritime companies striving to reduce their environmental footprint. By opting for sustainable packaging solutions, companies can significantly reduce waste and demonstrate a comprehensive commitment to sustainability.

One key aspect of this strategy involves selecting packaging materials that are recyclable, biodegradable, or made from renewable resources. These choices minimise the environmental impact throughout the product's lifecycle, from production to disposal. Additionally, it's crucial to communicate the adoption of green packaging and materials effectively. This can be done through marketing materials, highlighting the company's dedication to minimising its ecological impact.

Product labels are another valuable platform for conveying this commitment to customers, allowing them to make informed choices and support sustainable practices. In essence, green packaging and materials are not just an environmentally responsible choice but also a tangible expression of a company's commitment to reducing waste and contributing to a greener future.

11. TARGETED ADVERTISING:

In digital marketing, tailoring advertising campaigns to reach eco-conscious audiences is a strategic move for maritime companies committed to sustainability. This involves customising ad copy and visuals to emphasise the company's green initiatives and positive environmental impact.

One effective approach is to leverage digital advertising platforms that offer precise targeting options. Using demographic and behavioural data, companies can identify and engage with specific audience segments interested in sustainability. This allows for delivering tailored messages that resonate with eco-conscious consumers, showcasing the company's commitment to environmentally responsible practices. Furthermore, such targeted advertising ensures that marketing efforts are cost-effective and align with the intended audience's values and preferences. It's a way to connect with consumers who share the company's sustainability ethos, reinforcing the importance of green practices in the maritime industry.

12. CUSTOMER LOYALTY PROGRAMS:

Building customer loyalty among those who choose green shipping services is essential for maritime companies dedicated to sustainability. Implementing loyalty programs tailored to eco-conscious consumers can be a powerful strategy to achieve this goal.

These programs can reward and incentivise repeat customers by offering discounts on future shipments or eco-friendly perks, such as carbon offset options. By doing so, companies acknowledge and appreciate their customers' environmentally responsible choices and encourage them to continue making eco-conscious decisions. Moreover, loyalty programs can foster a sense of community among like-minded customers committed to sustainability. This sense of belonging can enhance the customer experience and strengthen their connection with the company, leading to higher customer retention rates and positive word-of-mouth referrals. In essence, customer loyalty programs designed with eco-consciousness are a win-win solution that benefits both customers and the maritime industry's sustainability efforts.

By implementing these marketing and branding strategies, green shipping companies can effectively communicate their commitment to sustainability, connect with like-minded customers, and contribute to the growth of eco-friendly practices in the maritime industry.

BUILDING TRUST AND LOYALTY THROUGH ECO-FRIENDLY PRACTICES

Building trust and loyalty through eco-friendly practices is a fundamental objective for green shipping companies. In an era where sustainability and environmental responsibility are at the forefront of consumer consciousness, companies that demonstrate a genuine commitment to these principles can establish stronger connections with their customers. By consistently adopting and promoting eco-friendly practices, shipping companies reduce their environmental impact and gain the trust of environmentally conscious consumers.

Transparency is key to building trust. Companies that openly communicate their sustainability initiatives, such as using alternative fuels, reducing emissions, and implementing green technologies, demonstrate a commitment to transparency. Customers appreciate knowing how their choices align with their values, and transparent communication fosters a sense of honesty and credibility.

Consistency in sustainable practices is equally important. Shipping companies that consistently adhere to green principles, even navigating complex logistics and operational challenges, signal their dedication to long-term sustainability. This consistency builds confidence in customers who seek reliability and ethical responsibility.

Customer education plays a pivotal role in the trust-building process. By providing information about the environmental benefits of eco-friendly shipping options and how these choices positively impact the planet, companies empower their customers to make informed decisions. Educated customers are more likely to become advocates for environmentally responsible shipping.

Loyalty is a natural byproduct of trust. When customers trust that a shipping company genuinely cares about environmental stewardship, they are likelier to remain loyal to that brand. Loyalty programs that reward eco-conscious choices, discounts for repeat green shipping or exclusive access to sustainable products and services can further solidify customer commitment.

Ultimately, green shipping companies prioritising eco-friendly practices and actively engaging with their customers on sustainability-related topics are well-positioned to build trust and foster lasting loyalty. This trust enhances customer retention and contributes to the broader goals of sustainability and environmental preservation.

Chapter 20

CONCLUSION AND CALL TO ACTION

In this comprehensive exploration of green shipping, we have embarked on a journey through the maritime industry's transformation toward sustainability, innovation, and responsibility. We've uncovered the complex interplay of environmental, economic, and social factors that shape the maritime landscape. As we draw this book to a close, it is essential to reflect on the profound significance of the maritime sector's commitment to green practices and the call to action for all stakeholders involved.

SUMMARISING KEY TAKEAWAYS FROM THE BOOK

Throughout this book, we have explored the multifaceted world of green shipping, uncovering key takeaways that encapsulate the industry's transformation towards sustainability and responsible practices:

ENVIRONMENTAL IMPERATIVE

The maritime industry's pivot toward renewable energy and sustainability is a strategic choice and a vital response to the pressing environmental imperative. For decades, conventional shipping practices have significantly affected the Earth's ecosystems. The industry's heavy reliance on fossil fuels has contributed to air and water pollution, greenhouse gas emissions, oil spills, and habitat destruction. This environmental impact has raised ecological concerns and generated public outrage and regulatory scrutiny. As a result, there is an urgent need for greener and more responsible alternatives in maritime shipping. Embracing renewable energy sources and sustainable practices is crucial to mitigating the industry's environmental footprint and addressing the global climate crisis.

EVOLUTION OF MARITIME SHIPPING

To truly appreciate the significance of the maritime industry's transition toward sustainability, it's essential to consider the historical context of shipping. For centuries, shipping primarily relied on fossil fuels, particularly heavy oil and diesel, due to their energy density and availability. This long-standing tradition served as the backbone of global trade and transportation. However, the maritime sector is at a crossroads as the world grapples with climate change and environmental degradation. The industry's evolution, driven by technological advancements and a growing awareness of environmental challenges, has laid the groundwork for this transformative journey. It reflects the industry's adaptability and commitment to forging a more sustainable and responsible path forward. Understanding this evolution provides valuable insights into the challenges and opportunities that lie ahead as maritime shipping embraces renewable energy and sustainable practices to meet the demands of the 21st century.

SUSTAINABLE DESIGN AND RETROFITTING

The adoption of sustainable ship designs and the retrofitting of existing vessels represent significant milestones in the maritime industry's quest for eco-friendliness. Sustainable ship design involves creating vessels with reduced environmental footprints, incorporating features like advanced propulsion systems, efficient hull designs, and emission-reduction technologies. Retrofitting existing ships to align with green standards is another commendable effort. Successful case studies underscore the industry's commitment to embracing cleaner technologies and practices. These transformations improve a vessel's environmental performance and inspire confidence in the maritime sector's ability to adapt to a more sustainable future. They are tangible examples of how innovative engineering and a conscientious approach can contribute to a greener and more responsible maritime industry.

ECONOMICS OF GREEN SHIPPING

One of the central drivers behind the maritime industry's shift toward sustainability lies in the economics of green shipping. A thorough cost-benefit analysis reveals that investing in eco-friendly technologies and practices can yield substantial long-term financial benefits. While the initial investment in green initiatives may seem significant, it often leads to lower operational costs over time. Additionally, government incentives and subsidies further encourage the adoption of sustainable solutions. These financial incentives can offset the costs of transitioning to renewable energy sources, emissions reduction measures, and eco-friendly ship designs. The economic viability of green shipping is increasingly evident, demonstrating that sustainability is not only an ethical choice but a sound financial decision. It underscores the industry's recognition that embracing environmentally responsible practices can lead to profitability and a more sustainable future for global maritime transportation.

ENVIRONMENTAL REGULATIONS

The maritime industry's commitment to sustainability is intricately tied to its compliance with a complex web of international and national environmental regulations. This aspect highlights the industry's recognition of its environmental responsibilities. Regulations governing air emissions, ballast water management, and reducing greenhouse gases have been established to address the sector's environmental impact. Understanding the legal ramifications of non-compliance underscores the necessity of adhering to these environmental standards. The maritime industry acknowledges that failure to meet these regulations results in penalties and fines and has far-reaching ecological consequences. The strict adherence to these rules is a testament to the industry's commitment to mitigating its environmental impact and embracing more sustainable practices.

ENVIRONMENTAL IMPACT ASSESSMENT

The maritime industry's journey toward sustainability is significantly influenced by rigorous environmental impact assessment methods. These approaches, such as life cycle assessment and performance indicators, play a pivotal role in evaluating the industry's environmental footprint and identifying opportunities for improvement. Life cycle assessment examines the full spectrum of environmental impacts associated with maritime operations, from ship construction to operation and eventual decommissioning. Performance indicators, on the other hand, provide measurable metrics to gauge a vessel's efficiency and environmental performance. By utilising these assessment tools, the maritime sector can systematically analyse its ecological footprint, pinpoint areas that require intervention, and monitor progress toward sustainability goals. These methods are indispensable for ensuring that the industry's sustainability efforts are data-driven, accountable, and effective in reducing its environmental impact.

MONITORING AND MITIGATION

The maritime industry's commitment to sustainability is accompanied by a suite of advanced technologies and practices designed to comprehensively monitor and mitigate its environmental impact. These include air emissions, water quality, noise pollution, ecological assessments, and social impact evaluations. Air emission monitoring systems are deployed to measure and manage emissions of pollutants like sulphur oxides (SOx), nitrogen oxides (NOx), and particulate matter (PM), ensuring compliance with stringent regulations. Water quality assessments are essential for maintaining the health of aquatic ecosystems by managing ballast water and minimising the risk of invasive species introduction. Noise pollution studies address the acoustic impact of maritime activities on marine life, aiming to reduce disturbances to underwater environments. Ecological surveys and social impact assessments consider the broader consequences of shipping operations, ensuring that environmental conservation and community well-being are integral components of the industry's sustainability agenda. This multifaceted approach to monitoring and mitigation underscores the industry's dedication to minimising its ecological footprint while advancing sustainable practices.

TECHNOLOGICAL ADVANCES

Technological innovation is at the forefront of the maritime industry's efforts to achieve sustainability. Pioneering developments in clean propulsion systems and renewable energy solutions have become pivotal in reducing emissions and enhancing environmental sustainability. These advancements include the adoption of alternative fuels such as liquefied natural gas (LNG) and hydrogen, which substantially reduce greenhouse gas emissions compared to traditional bunker fuels. Additionally, the integration of wind-assisted propulsion systems and solar panels harnesses renewable energy sources, contributing to reduced reliance on conventional fossil fuels. Electric and hybrid propulsion systems further enhance efficiency and decrease emissions. These technological strides underscore the industry's recognition of innovation's critical role in minimising its environmental impact and ushering in a greener era of maritime shipping.

EFFICIENCY IMPROVEMENTS

Sustainable shipping practices extend beyond vessel propulsion and encompass the entire supply chain. The industry recognises that optimising efficiency along this intricate network is critical to reducing fuel consumption and emissions. Technology and operational planning advancements are pivotal in achieving these efficiency gains. From demand forecasting and just-in-time inventory management to route optimisation and cargo handling automation, the maritime sector continually refines its practices to minimise energy consumption and environmental impact. These efficiency improvements reflect the industry's commitment to a holistic approach to sustainability, where every link in the supply chain contributes to reducing greenhouse gas emissions and an eco-friendlier future.

ECONOMIC VIABILITY

Environmental imperatives and economic considerations drive the maritime industry's transition to sustainable practices. Detailed cost-effectiveness and return on investment analyses have underscored the financial advantages of embracing sustainability. Shipping companies increasingly recognise that sustainable measures can be economically viable, leading to reduced operational costs in the long term. Investments in green technologies, alternative fuels, and energy-efficient vessels often translate into significant savings through reduced fuel consumption and lower emissions. These findings reinforce the industry's belief that sustainability and profitability are not mutually exclusive but can coexist harmoniously. Thus, the maritime sector is increasingly motivated to adopt eco-conscious practices that benefit the planet and contribute to the industry's economic well-being.

SUSTAINABLE PORT INFRASTRUCTURE

The maritime industry recognises that achieving sustainability goals goes beyond vessels and extends to the ports and infrastructure that support maritime operations. Ports facilitate renewable energy integration and reduce the industry's carbon footprint. Investments in sustainable port infrastructure, such as shore power facilities that enable vessels to connect to clean electricity while berthed, reduce emissions and contribute to the overall sustainability of the shipping sector. These developments underscore the interconnectedness of various elements within the maritime ecosystem and emphasise the industry's commitment to adopting holistic solutions encompassing maritime operations and supporting infrastructure.

LOGISTICS AND EFFICIENCY

Sustainability efforts within the maritime industry extend well beyond the boundaries of ships and ports. Sustainable logistics practices and efficiency improvements are essential to the industry's commitment to reducing emissions and enhancing operational efficiency. Advanced technologies like real-time cargo tracking, predictive analytics, and data-driven decision-making allow shipping companies to optimise cargo loading, unloading, and transport routes, ultimately minimising energy consumption and environmental impact. The industry's focus on efficiency is a response to environmental concerns and a strategic effort to maximise resource utilisation and reduce operational costs. By embracing sustainable logistics and efficient practices, the maritime sector is dedicated to achieving a more eco-friendly and economically viable future.

ENERGY STORAGE AND MANAGEMENT

Integrating renewable energy sources into maritime operations heavily relies on adequate energy storage and management systems. To harness the potential of wind, solar, or hybrid propulsion systems, ships require advanced energy storage solutions like batteries or flywheels. These systems store excess energy when available, enabling vessels to operate efficiently even when renewable sources aren't generating power. Additionally, energy management systems optimise power distribution on board, reducing energy waste and ensuring the efficient use of generators. The maritime industry's emphasis on energy storage and management highlights its determination to embrace innovative technologies that reduce emissions and enhance sustainability while maintaining reliable operations.

ENVIRONMENTAL REPORTING AND ACCOUNTABILITY

As part of its commitment to sustainability, the maritime industry recognises the significance of transparency, reporting requirements, and accountability mechanisms. Accurate and detailed environmental reporting, including emissions data and fuel consumption records, is essential for demonstrating compliance with international and national regulations. Moreover, such reporting fosters accountability to stakeholders, including customers, investors, and regulatory bodies. By openly sharing sustainability progress and adhering to rigorous reporting standards, the maritime sector reinforces its dedication to environmental responsibility. It builds trust with those invested in its journey toward greener practices.

CLIMATE CHANGE IMPACT

Climate change poses significant challenges to the maritime shipping industry, affecting everything from vessel operations to port infrastructure. Rising sea levels, extreme weather events, and shifting ocean currents can disrupt maritime routes and port facilities, increasing risks for shipping companies. Understanding these impacts is critical for the industry's long-term resilience. Strategies to mitigate climate-related risks involve vessel design enhancements, infrastructure improvements, and route planning adjustments that account for changing environmental conditions. The maritime sector's proactive approach to addressing climate change underscores its commitment to sustainability and its willingness to adapt to an evolving world.

PUBLIC PERCEPTION AND CONSUMER DEMAND

Public perception and consumer demand are potent drivers of change in the maritime industry. As society becomes increasingly environmentally conscious, people expect responsible practices from shipping companies. This shift in awareness and values compels the industry to engage with transparency, clear communication, and eco-friendly branding strategies. Shipping companies that align with these evolving preferences and prioritise sustainability can gain a competitive edge, foster customer loyalty, and contribute to a greener future. It's a testament to the industry's adaptability and willingness to meet the expectations of a more environmentally conscious global community.

GLOBAL COLLABORATION

Achieving sustainability in the maritime industry requires a global effort. International initiatives, collaborative partnerships, and coordinated actions are vital for addressing the industry's environmental challenges. Organisations like the International Maritime Organisation (IMO) are pivotal in setting international standards and regulations for greener shipping practices. Furthermore, the industry's stakeholders, including governments, shipping companies, and environmental organisations, must work together to drive meaningful change. By fostering global collaboration, the maritime sector can collectively reduce its environmental impact, optimise resource utilisation, and contribute to a more sustainable future for the planet.

FUTURE TRENDS

The maritime industry is evolving rapidly, driven by emerging technologies and a clear commitment to sustainable practices. Predictions for green shipping indicate a future where vessels are powered by alternative fuels like hydrogen or ammonia, equipped with state-of-the-art emissions control systems, and harnessing renewable energy sources for propulsion. Innovation in ship design, propulsion systems, and logistics management will continue to shape the industry's future. As the world transitions toward cleaner energy sources and stricter environmental regulations, the maritime sector's proactive approach to embracing these trends ensures its long-term viability and competitiveness. The industry paves the way for a greener and more eco-conscious maritime future by staying at the forefront of technological advancements and sustainability initiatives.

ENVIRONMENTAL RESPONSIBILITY

Establishing trust and cultivating customer loyalty go hand in hand with a solid commitment to environmental responsibility. As consumers increasingly prioritise sustainability, maritime companies can build lasting relationships by demonstrating their dedication to eco-friendly practices. This responsibility extends beyond regulatory compliance and underscores the industry's role in safeguarding the environment. By consistently delivering on their sustainability promises, shipping companies can attract environmentally conscious consumers and retain their trust and loyalty. These practices benefit the planet and contribute to the industry's long-term success.

CALL TO ACTION

The journey towards a sustainable and responsible maritime industry requires a collective call to action. This call emphasises the importance of collaboration, innovation, and unwavering commitment to a greener future. It beckons shipping companies, governments, stakeholders, and consumers to work together to reduce emissions, protect marine ecosystems, and foster sustainable practices. By answering this call, the maritime sector can lead by example, inspiring other industries to follow suit. Through shared goals, meaningful partnerships, and a united vision, the industry can set a precedent for environmental responsibility that extends far beyond its waters, contributing to a more sustainable world for future generations.

These key takeaways underscore the urgency and potential of green shipping in contributing to a sustainable planet, resilient economies, and a thriving maritime sector that respects environmental stewardship. The journey toward a greener maritime industry is ongoing, and the call to action resonates with all stakeholders, from industry leaders to consumers, to collectively navigate this transformative path.

REINFORCING THE IMPORTANCE OF EMBRACING RENEWABLE ENERGY

Reinforcing the importance of embracing renewable energy in maritime shipping cannot be overstated in today's world. The urgency of addressing climate change, reducing greenhouse gas emissions, and protecting fragile marine ecosystems demands a swift and resolute transition to sustainable practices within the industry. The environmental consequences of conventional shipping, characterised by the use of fossil fuels and high emissions, have brought the sector under intense scrutiny. Embracing renewable energy through cleaner fuels, innovative propulsion systems, or energy-efficient designs represents a pivotal shift towards environmental responsibility.

Beyond the environmental imperative, compelling economic and social reasons exist to prioritise renewable energy adoption. Sustainable shipping practices can lead to cost savings, operational efficiency, and long-term financial benefits for companies investing in green technologies. Moreover, consumers and stakeholders increasingly demand transparency and accountability from the maritime industry, aligning their preferences with environmentally responsible companies.

The global call to action, reflected in international and national regulations, collaborative initiatives, and shifting consumer behaviours, underscores the industry's pivotal role in global sustainability efforts. The maritime sector must heed this call and, in doing so, contribute not only to environmental preservation but also to the creation of a more resilient, efficient, and sustainable future. Embracing renewable energy is not merely an option but an ethical and strategic imperative for the maritime industry to thrive in an environmentally conscious and economically competitive world.

URGING COLLECTIVE ACTION AND CONTINUED INNOVATION IN THE MARITIME SHIPPING SECTOR

Urging collective action and continued innovation in the maritime shipping sector is a clarion call to address today's pressing challenges and opportunities. Environmental, economic, and social factors complexity necessitates a united effort among all stakeholders, from shipping companies and governments to consumers and researchers.

Collective action is essential because the maritime sector's impact extends beyond its immediate operations. It influences global trade, climate change, and the well-being of coastal communities. Collaboration among nations, organisations, and industries is paramount in setting ambitious sustainability goals, shaping international regulations, and fostering a culture of environmental responsibility.

Continued innovation is the lifeblood of the industry's transformation. Developing clean propulsion systems, energy-efficient logistics, and sustainable port infrastructure is crucial to reducing emissions and environmental impact. Technological advancements also increase operational efficiency, translating into economic benefits for shipping companies.

Moreover, the maritime sector must remain adaptive and responsive to the evolving expectations of consumers and stakeholders. Environmental awareness and demand for eco-friendly shipping services are growing. To meet these demands, the industry must embrace existing green technologies and push the boundaries of innovation.

As the maritime sector charts its course into the future, the call for collective action and innovation echoes as a guiding principle. The challenges are formidable, but so too are the opportunities. By working together, embracing innovation, and staying committed to sustainability, the maritime shipping sector can not only navigate the complexities of our time but also emerge as a beacon of responsible global trade and environmental stewardship.

www.ingramcontent.com/pod-product-compliance
Lightning Source LLC
LaVergne TN
LVHW062318070526
838202LV00051B/4127